Fortnite For Kids

3 Books in 1

Underground Tips & Secrets To Become

a Fortnite God & Win Battle Royale LIKE

THE PRO's

D0360882

By

Pro Gamer Guide

2018

The following book is reproduced below with the goal of providing information that is as accurate and reliable as possible. Regardless, purchasing this eBook can be seen as consent to the fact that both the publisher and the author of this book are in no way experts on the topics discussed within and that any recommendations or suggestions that are made herein are for entertainment purposes only. Professionals should be consulted as needed prior to undertaking any of the action endorsed herein.

This declaration is deemed fair and valid by both the American Bar Association and the Committee of Publishers Association and is legally binding throughout the United States.

Furthermore, the transmission, duplication or reproduction of any of the following work including specific information will be considered an illegal act irrespective of if it is done electronically or in print. This extends to creating a secondary or tertiary copy of the work or a recorded copy and is only allowed with the express written consent from the Publisher. All additional right reserved.

The information in the following pages is broadly considered to be a truthful and accurate account of facts and as such any inattention, use or misuse of the information in question by the reader will render any resulting actions solely under their purview. There are no scenarios in which the publisher or the original author of this work can be in any fashion deemed liable for any hardship or damages that may befall them after undertaking information described herein.

Additionally, the information in the following pages is intended only for informational purposes and should thus be thought of as universal. As befitting its nature, it is presented without assurance regarding its prolonged validity or interim quality. Trademarks that are mentioned are done without written consent and can in no way be considered an endorsement from the trademark holder.

Learn the latest tricks and tips while you play!

Get this this 3 book 1 bundle complete audiobook for absolutely **FREE**, and get access to Underground Tips & Secrets To Become a Fortnite God & Win Battle Royale LIKE THE PRO'S!

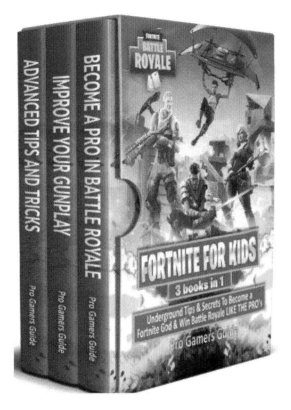

Download it for free: <u>adbl.co/2PQHdX3</u>

Table of Contents

Book – I

Book - II 78

Book - III

Book – I

Fortnite: Battle Royale

Become a Pro in Battle Royale with Secret Building, Combat Strategies, Hidden Chests, and More!

By

Pro Gamer Guide

Introduction

Congratulations on downloading *Fortnite: Become a Pro in Battle Royale with Secret Building, Combat Strategies, Hidden Chests, and More!* Thank you for doing so.

The following chapters will discuss in great detail what it will take to become a Fortnite pro, with chapters covering what it means to be a pro at this popular game, everything involved in building in the world of Fortnite, all-important "must-know" strategies for any serious gamer, the ins and outs of ramp rushing and gaining the high ground, the best approach to attacking bases, a review of the many weapons available in Fortnite and some thoughts on how to best employ them, and a list of some of the secrets in the game, such as hidden chest locations and victory drops.

There are plenty of books on this subject on the market, so thanks again for choosing this one! Every effort was made to ensure it is full of as much useful information as possible. Please enjoy!

Chapter 1
Becoming A Fortnite Pro

Fortnite: Battle Royale

If you're reading this, you're undoubtedly aware of the worldwide gaming phenomenon that is **Fortnite: Battle Royale**. Everyone is. Fortnite has risen beyond being a popular game to being a major cultural milestone. It's played and loved by everyone from middle school through adulthood, and people are obsessed, playing for countless hours, consuming endless live streams, talking Fortnite, learning the Fortnite lingo, and living Fortnite. After a somewhat difficult initial roll-out, Fortnite has caught fire, and the appeal is pretty obvious. One advantage it has over similar games (such as PUBG) is that it is free. The game itself—everything significant used for gameplay—all free. It's also playable across multiple platforms. And the one element of gameplay that makes for a truly unique experience is the way it incorporates building into combat. Right now, there's nothing bigger in the gaming world than Fortnite and it shows no signs of giving up the top spot.

What is a pro?

"Become a pro." It's in the title. What does it mean to be a pro? A professional? In the real world, you have achieved professional when you are paid to do a job. The broader meaning and the one that is relevant in this context is that being a pro means that you have been trained to do your job and to do it well. If you're a serious gamer, you know what this means. You might not take a course or have a mentor, but you spend countless hours of largely self-guided training, building up your ability to become an expert. No, you're probably not going to be playing **Fortnite: Battle Royale** for money, but you want to learn to play it *as if you were* getting paid for it. You want to have the same tools you'd have if it were your job.

And what kind of job would that be? What profession does the experience of playing Fortnite most closely resemble? Being really good at this game is kind of like being a professional athlete in that you'll rely on split-second decision-making and finely-honed reflexes, but even more relevant, given the subject-matter, it's like being a soldier. With that in mind, the three things you need to build in order to be a good Fortnite player are Strategy, Intel, and Skill.

The Tools

Strategy

A strategy is a plan you use to achieve a goal. More than anything, this book is designed to give you useful strategies for winning, methods to beat the opponents you encounter on the island. Consider it a playbook of plans and tactics you can use to outmaneuver, outplay, outthink and out-build your enemies. We'll cover a lot of strategies to use in different situations that you can learn and practice as you play.

Intel

Intel, short for intelligence, refers to information. Spies gather it and armies use it to tactical advantage on the battlefield. Particularly in the section on hidden chests and victory drops, this book will provide you with useful intel to give you a leg up on other players.

Skill

If you're a serious gamer—and I assume you are since you purchased an advanced strategy book—you already understand this step. Skill is something you develop through practice. It's the reason that they have basic training and maneuvers for soldiers, and that athletes practice every day, both in and out of season. If you know the basic moves of the game, you build skill by repeating them. It's like muscle memory. In the same way that a seasoned football player can throw a perfect spiral without thinking about all of the little steps involved in achieving it consciously, you can build your gameplay skills through practice, repeating until they're stored in your subconscious mind as muscle memory and you can access them faster, almost automatically. This is what they call being in the zone. When you're in the zone, you're relying on the skills you've built, not a conscious thinking yourself through the moves, and indeed, for top athletes, there's no faster way out of the zone than overthinking your athletic endeavors on a conscious level. Although this book will touch on skill here and there, this part is up to you. If you want to get better, you need to play. If you get used to using them, you will develop skills at using the strategies this book teaches. With practice, you'll find yourself building your speed and ability and employing different strategies almost automatically—and shutting down your enemies left and right.

Okay, now let's dive in!

Chapter 2
A Beginner's Guide to Building

Fortnite: Battle Royale is a survival/deathmatch game and as such your overarching goals when playing are actually pretty simple. On the most basic level, your goal is to survive. You'll be diving in using your hang-glider (or the umbrella once you've achieved your first victory) to land on the island with up to a hundred other players and the game will continue until only one of you is left alive. No matter what else you do, if you're the last man standing, you've won. In service of that goal, gameplay, and your strategy, consists of gathering weapons (the best and most strategically useful you can find), looting, and doing whatever else you need to in order to prevail over the other players. The other wrinkle is that there is a shrinking circle of the storm's eye, a safe zone that functionally limits your ability to explore. Functionally, this serves as the ticking clock of the game. Outside is a storm that will slowly kill you. The gradually shrinking size of the circle inexorably forces survivors into closer and closer proximity to each other, thus increasing the likelihood of combat. Although the goals are simple, the fact that you will be interacting with a many other unpredictable players keeps the game intense. If you want to survive, you need strong building strategies. First, let's cover the basics of building within the game.

You need supplies in order to build. Building supplies come in three types: metal, brick and wood. Metal is the hardest to find but the most resistant to damage and thus the best source of protection. Wood is easiest to find (trees are everywhere) but the least resistant. It is best used for exploring the world, constructing stairs, ramps and bridges, but is not a good choice for bases or other fortifications. Brick splits the difference between the other two materials: harder to find than wood but tougher, easier to find than metal but also weaker. Consider bricks your backup for metal when fortifying your position. Wood is the fastest for building, whereas bricks and metal both take a little longer.

There are two ways to procure these materials. One is to mine them from the environment using your pickaxe. You can use it on anything in the world, from structures to rocks to trees to vehicles, breaking these items down into usable building supplies. Using vehicles as your supply for metal is a particularly effective strategy, especially if you focus your gathering areas on the cities on the map which have more available automobiles to strip. Supplies can also be found randomly among other items at loot spots. Supplies don't count against available space in your backpack, so you don't have to concern yourself with allowing room for them.

A good strategy is to stock up on supplies early in the game before the eye of the storm forces you into smaller and smaller areas. Supplies will be more plentiful when the safe zone is wider and you'll be better able to mine and gather with a relatively lower density of opponents. Using your pickaxe makes noise, so it's a riskier proposition once survivors have been forced into a more constrained space. It's a good idea as you explore the island to keep gathering supplies in the back of your head and when you see opportunities, especially early in the game to farm supplies when the opportunity presents itself. It can take a bit of time, can alert enemies to your presence, and can be a distraction from possible dangers, but it needs to be done. If you are going to survive the final conflict, you'll need to have a significant stash of building supplies to work with while fortifying your position.

Assuming you've gathered sufficient supplies, the first step in building is to open up your blueprints. You can do this by pressing the F1 through F5 buttons on your PC keyboard, pressing the B button on the Xbox, or Circle on the PS4. Once they are opened, a semi-transparent version of the structure will appear. It is a preview of what it will look like when placed. You can rotate these by pressing R on your keyboard or the right bumper on one of the console systems. If you want to change which of your building supplies you are using, you can do this by pressing the right mouse button on your keyboard or the left bumper on a console. If you're satisfied, you can place your structure by clicking the left button on the mouse or the right trigger on a console. To go into edit mode once you've placed a structure, press G on a keyboard, B on Xbox, or the circle on a PS4. Pieces can be removed by left clicking on a keyboard or using the right trigger on consoles, and then you may leave edit mode, thus confirming changes, by once again pressing G on your keyboard, B on Xbox, or circle on a PS4.

These are the steps you use to build structures. Your options include walls, ceilings, stairs, ramps, and other options. Once you get the hang of it, it becomes intuitive quickly, and it's easy to build elaborate structures because the pieces all naturally snap together.

There are several basic ways to use building to your advantage in the field. You can make a small structure to give yourself cover and a place to hide, or you can build yourself a base. A common strategy is to build towering bases to give yourself the height advantage over your enemies, and you can place traps to further this advantage. Once strategic point to keep in mind: no matter the size of the base, it is dependent on a strong foundation. If an enemy takes out your foundation, the entire structure will collapse. This is something to keep in mind when you're standing atop a massive structure and enjoying your height advantage. Don't get arrogant and remember that all it takes is a well-placed rocket to bring it all crashing down and take you immediately out of the competition. Fortunes can be reversed in an instant in Fortnite: Battle Royale and the smart player never lets a moment of earned success blind him to all of the hungry opponents that are constantly gunning for him.

You can also build while on the run, placing walls behind you to give you cover from enemy fire. One thing to keep in mind when in this situation is that it takes new walls a few seconds to completely build. They'll immediately give you visual cover, but until they solidify they are very susceptible to destruction by enemy fire.

On the most basic level, this describes the basic building elements as they function within gameplay in Fortnite: Battle Royale. But this knowledge alone gives you no advantage. These are the tools all players will be using, except for possibly the extremely inexperienced. To give you an advantage over your enemies, you need stronger building strategies, which we will cover in the second half of the chapter. First, though, I want to briefly cover the turbo building mode, and when to use it and when not to.

Turbo Building

The turbo building mode was somewhat controversial among **Fortnite** enthusiasts when it was first launched in the 3.0 patch. Some thought it made the game too easy, and others found it glitchy. The glitches have been smoothed out over subsequent patches, and it now can enable very fast and very intuitive building.

So, what does turbo mode do, exactly? It's a mode that is on as a default, although it can be turned off if you prefer the original build mode (described in the first section). Turbo mode gives you the option to hold down the mouse button, or whatever build button you're using on your console (see above) and build while you are turning and moving. Basically, it leaves you in a state of constant building while it is engaged and builds along your path as you move through the world.

The big advantage this gives over the original build mode is that you don't have to click on every single piece you want to place. It's easy to see where this could be advantageous. Time is always at a premium while playing **Fortnite**. If you've slowed down to build, you're theoretically leaving yourself open to attack while distracted. Being able to erect whatever structure you have in mind more quickly is a distinct tactical advantage: it leaves you open to attack for a shorter amount of time.

If, for example, you want to place a 1x1 wall around yourself, you can just hold down whichever build button your system uses and rotate 360 degrees. Whereas before you'd lose precious seconds stopping to click each piece into place, they now drop down as you spin instantaneously. Another example in which you can see this advantage is if you are double-ramping up a mountain. Before, if you wanted to build parallel ramps up a mountain, you had to do some complex maneuvering and clicking to keep both ramps going. With turbo engaged, you just steer your character dodging back and forth in a serpentine movement as he or she travels up the building ramp and it automatically lays it down. Like I said, it is a tool that becomes intuitive very quickly with practice.

As for the controversy: there were voices within the fan community saying it had ruined the game when the turbo mode was first launched, but those voices have largely died out in the months since its rollout. This is a pretty common phenomenon. People complain when something new upsets the version they've learned. This version was designed to even the playing field for new players, allowing them to build more quickly before they'd had time to develop the skills that players who'd trained on the earlier version had already acquired. Naturally, this rubbed some veteran players the wrong way. But like I said, the voices of complaint quickly died out. It's possible some of them left the game in protest, but I suspect most of them got used to the new version and just got over it. In any case, I think it's a cool function. It *does* even the playing field, deemphasizing speed of building. As it has this effect, it makes strategy all that much more important.

Pro Building Tips

Okay, now that we've covered the basic mechanics of building, let's get into some strategy. Some of this was alluded to in the examples of the above section, but the following section will tie the steps you will be performing to tactical decision-making.

The most basic structure in Fortnite is the 1x1 room. Some people call this a panic building or panic walls. If you're taking fire, you can quickly put up a 1x1 around yourself for protection from the bullets. We mentioned these when discussing turbo mode. If you're using turbo mode, simply spinning in a circle with the wall selected from your structure options while turbo is engaged will quickly place a panic building around your character.

Typically, once you've created this protected area, you might consider installing a ramp in order to gain the high ground. You'll hear players refer to this height advantage frequently, and this isn't something unique to this game, or games in general. This is tactics 101. The concept was formalized in the fifth century BC by Sun Tzu in his seminal classic of tactics, *The Art of War*, which has been studied by generals and military students worldwide. In *The Art of War*, the leaders of armies are directed to strive to take the high ground, letting enemies attempt to attack from the disadvantaged lower point. The high ground gives you a broader field of view in which to view your enemies, unobstructed by valley walls and other structures that might interfere in lower positions. Consider snipers: they use this to their advantage. The combination of high ground and cover can make them virtually unassailable, allowing them to take out large numbers of enemies who might not even know where they are located.

In Fortnite, gaining the high ground can be accomplished by building a ramp (sometimes called a panic ramp, when included in panic walls). Choose the ramp from your menu and then either 1) jump while hitting the confirm button, or if you're in turbo mode 2) just jump as the ramp forms beneath you. Once you've done this, you've accomplished a basic tactical advantage, cover, and height. If you want to try a more ambitious version that will give more room to maneuver and better coverage on multiple sides, you can build a rectangular (rather than square) box with inward facing ramps that connect in the middle in a triangular arrangement.

This kind of functional panic buildings can be used early in the game during encounters with enemies, but as the safe zone contracts and players are forced into an ever tighter area, it's time to consider building a more elaborate fortification. It can be a mistake to build your base too early, as you might find yourself forced away from it by the storm, but there comes a point where it's down to a smaller number of players in a confined area, and a well-formed fort can make the difference between survival and death.

Before I get into this well-built fort, indulge me in a little tangent as I remind you of the overriding importance of survival in this game. It is the most important goal in Battle Royale, ultimately the only goal. It's all there in the title. It's a fight to the death. You're not gathering points for killing the most enemies. One player is rewarded, and that's the only one alive at the end. Personally, I advocate an active approach. Some players are timid and try to avoid detection until the later rounds. Find what works best for you, but if you're hiding, make sure it's a tactical choice and not out of a generally timid approach. You'll have to fight at some point, and you don't build skills by hiding. Another advantage to engaging with your opponents: although your survival is your primary goal and what makes the difference between victory and defeat, in killing opponents you give yourself access to everything they've gathered over the course of the game. This can provide you with ammunition, building materials, or superior firepower. So, even though eliminating enemies isn't strictly necessary to win the game, it is a practical necessity as it can, in many ways, give you a strategic advantage that you can exploit towards your ultimate goal of being the last survivor.

Okay, so the map has shrunk and it's time to build your fort. Remember to use durable material. Metal is the best, but depending on what supplies you gathered earlier in the game, a thoughtful combination of wood and brick can also work. Try to avoid using wood, as it is very easily destroyed by enemy fire. Start with the box and ramp described above (either version) then place a platform on top, leaping up to land on it as it falls into place. From there, it's a matter of repeating the pattern, adding stories to the building as you work your way up. Erecting walls and ramps within them until you've achieved the high ground over your enemies. A platform on top gives you a strong strategic point from which to attack your enemies with long-range weapons.

Another option is what gamers call a funnel fort. This is a raised structure with ramps projecting out from every side, thus creating a platform with a funnel shape. This gives you good options for offense or defense since you can achieve high ground by climbing up the ramps and shooting at your enemies, or hide inside the funnel for protection.

These are the basic base shapes, and for a lot of situations, you'll be doing variations on these. Sometimes, you just need to build a tall tower to get that height advantage, and speed and efficiency in your build can be more important than a clever design. Remember though, that any structure can be taken out by attacking the base, and if an enemy sneaks in under your radar, your high ground advantage will be useless if he manages to take your foundation out from under you, perhaps with the minigun. The whole structure will collapse and your character will fall to his or her death.

So far we've talked mostly panic walls and forts. In moment-to-moment gameplay, there are other ways you can use building. Ramps can be extremely useful for exploring the terrain, getting your character quickly into mountains or for climbing onto a structure. If you need to get down off a high perch, a cliff perhaps, you can create downward sloping ramps. Platforms can be used to make bridges extending from cliffs or connecting multiple structures. All of this is very easy to do, especially in turbo mode, and you can quickly gain skills at this.

Chapter 3
Advanced Building Strategies

Must-Know Strategies

In the previous chapter, we laid a foundation of basic strategies that can get you started. I want to now follow up with some strategies for specific situations. One thing you'll find when you play **Fortnite** is that the game is constantly changing in unpredictable ways. Since you're playing against others, often in large numbers that might be hunting you or destroying or creating structures, the world of the island is in constant flux. For this reason, you need flexible thinking and a toolbox of useful case-specific strategies you can pull out as needed. What follows are some strategies, many of them case-specific.

Building for Storms

So far, a lot of our building has been to avoid or thwart the dangers posed by other players. It can also be used to help achieve safety from the games other great threat: the storm. When the eye of the storm is contracting and the storm is closing in, you'll often find yourself in a position where you need to quickly escape from its path.

Sometimes, when doing this, the landscape itself can slow you down, sometimes enough to cause you harm. Building can help get you out of this trap. Instead of trying to flee at ground level, why not build up? You can use stairs or ramps to increase your elevation quickly and to avoid any pitfalls of the terrain, or bridges to quickly get across open spaces.

When Not To Build

Although building is a necessary part of the game, there are times that not building might be your best course of action. Consider this: it's usually pretty easy to spot a building that has been made by a player when compared to that pre-built within the game. Any player who has been around will be able to easily make this distinction. In cases like that, finding other sources of cover, those naturally occurring within the game-world, can actually be a pretty smart move. If such cover is nearby, you can quickly get behind it without calling a lot of attention to yourself by erecting a structure. This approach also has the advantage of allowing your weapons ready rather than getting distracted working with supplies. This strategy might not work in every situation—for example, if cover is not available. But all of these strategies are situation-specific. Use them when they'll help.

Building to Access Treasure Chests

Not all treasure is conveniently located on the ground waiting to be snatched up.

Some are placed in difficult to access places. There will be times you'll receive the hints of nearby treasure (the glow of the box or the characteristic mysterious tone). Sometimes this means using your pickaxe to smash through a wall. At others, you might have to build stairs or a ramp to quickly get to it.

Maximizing Your Building Speed

Chances are, many of your structures will be simple ones, built that way for pragmatic reasons. This will be true of your opponent as well. Given that, the outcome of conflicts will at times be determined by speed/skill. Using turbo mode helps, but another thing you can do to increase the speed at which you can effectively build is to increase the sensitivity of your controllers. You can do this by going into your settings. It can be a mistake to immediately max out the sensitivity. A more sensitive controller effectively changes the device you're using into one that reacts more quickly, and you need to be able to adjust to the new settings. Think of it like a car. If you're used to driving a clunker, and old car without power steering that takes a bit of muscle to steer into a steep curve, and then switch to a top of the line sports car with highly sensitive steering, the change is initially going to be off-putting. The reactions that you've trained into your body by driving the clunker and not going to serve you well on the better car. You'll tend to oversteer, especially when you need to react to something quickly. In time, you'll adjust.

Your **Fortnite** controllers are the same way. Increasing your sensitivity, eventually maxing it out, is a good idea, but to avoid losing control in the transitions, I recommend gradually increasing. When you feel skilled at the current level, move the sensitivity up one or two points until you grow accustomed to this new version, then up it again. After a while, you can have your sensitivity maxed and will know that your fastest building will be supported by your mouse or controller. Bear in mind that *your* max might not be the system's max. Find the spot that is most optimal for your reflexes and reaction time. This will serve you well in your shooting game, but also in quick building.

Building Walls on the Fly

Ideally, if you're building fortifications you're doing so with the luxury of a moment of respite, with no enemies breathing down your neck. But as anyone who has actually played the game knows, this is nothing you can count on. Enemies are everywhere and unpredictable.

They're unpredictable because they're real. If they were computer-generated, it's far more likely they'd have programmed and repetitive behavior that you could learn and, over time, counter, but they are being controlled by real, unpredictable, and flawed human beings like yourself. They can pop up anywhere and at any time and their behavior might not always be what you expect. It might not always even make sense. Don't expect them to do what you would. That being said, when they *do* pop up, and you haven't had the chance to build and there's nothing handy to hide behind, building on the fly is a great technique to help get yourself out of trouble. If you're suddenly being fired upon, throwing up a simple wall between you and your attacker can be a good step. Wood is your best option here because it solidifies the most quickly out of your material options. Once the wall is up, you have some cover and can take quick looks out from behind it to try to locate your enemy. Another option, once your wall is up, is to use the edit function to add a window or door that you can use to look out. If you can't immediately spot your opponent once you have cover, there's a good possibility you will be able to simply by their continued gunfire and visually tracking the path of the bullets.

Building Stairs or Ramps on the Fly

Another option when you're under fire is to build a set of stairs. This method entails more risk than building a wall and should only be used if you can see your attacker and are relatively close. Build up and carefully move up in a crouched position.

You can use the stairs for cover (although they won't provide as much as a wall) and can function to give you a height advantage from which to eliminate your enemy. In a variation, you can place multiple sets of stairs to throw off your opponent.

When the Storm is Closing In

As the game approaches its climax, the safe zone will have shrunk down to a very small circle, pushing surviving opponents into very close proximity with one another. At this point, players begin using up their surplus materials to fortify their positions. As mentioned earlier, you want to use metal or brick. As the end is near, there is no reason to worry about saving material at this point. You'll want to build quickly, preferably something with some height but pretty contained in its other dimensions. Build your tower upward, layering walls, stairs, and floors. I'd repeat the warning of not building up too high. If your foundation is knocked out from under you and you've built up too high, you might die in the subsequent fall. Another pro tip: you can repair your base by highlighting the damaged piece and pressing F on your keyboard or pressing down on the right button on a console system.

Setting Traps

Related to building is your capacity to set traps. It is easy, especially for beginners, to neglect this aspect of the game in favor of combat and building. This would be a big mistake. Trap setting is an important strategic tool and if you ignore it you are unnecessarily ceding an advantage to your opponents. As competitive as the world of **Fortnite: Battle Royale** is, you can't afford to give up any potential advantage.

It can easily make the difference between victory and failure. So, setting traps is an element you need to explore. To put it in the terms we discussed at the beginning of the book, you need to learn and develop strategies for setting traps (we'll address that here) and also build skills by doing it.

Earlier versions of traps, some of which were glitchy or of limited utility (including the ceiling zapper) have been removed from the game and consolidated into the damage trap. If a player steps on the damage trap, spikes will spring out and impale the player. These are easy to use. Once you're in building mode, select the trap slot and aim at the wall, ceiling, or floor. If the trap is highlighted in blue you have aimed at a spot where it can be placed. If it's red, you'll need to find another spot.

There are three main reasons that players sometimes hesitate to use traps. They require patience, it can be difficult to get other players to walk into them and they are survivable—they deliver 75 points of damage. For this reason, it is often a good idea to place a secondary trap to finish off your victim depending on the situation. Traps require ingenuity and perhaps appeal to a certain mindset. When pulled off well, they can add drama and surprise to the game and deliver you a win when your opponent least expects it. Let's talk about strategies.

On a basic level, traps can be placed to protect your base, placed in areas where you think enemies might go and that you'd rather they wouldn't. But traps work best when you build in stronger incentives.

One tried and true method is using loot as bait. Hiding a trap among a cache of loot can lure victims in. If properly placed, the loot might look like it is leftover from a previous kill. Combining the loot lure with building can be effective. Creating a building with windows or other openings that allow outside players to see within, then including loot as a lure can be effective. Other players might see the shiny lure and then wander in and trip the trap. Of course, it's also possible they may attach the structure and avoid falling for the trap. One of the tricks of traps is that they rely on the behavior of other players, which can be unpredictable. I see this as both the challenge and the fun of traps. It's fun to put yourself in the head of other players, trying to guess their thought process and outsmart them. It's the classic game of cat and mouse. They might not always behave as you'd anticipated, but when they do, a kill brought on by a triggered trap can be massively rewarding.

A variation on the loot trap within a structure is to build a series of multiple little houses. Little huts, really, with loot visible through the windows. Leave all but one of the huts unprotected. This can play on the psychology of other players. If they go for one of the unprotected huts first, they might lower their guard to the trap placed in one of the others.

Think of it this way, if you, in one way or another, are funneling the movement of your opponent down into a relatively small area, giving them fewer options of where to stand, you're increasing the likelihood they'll step on your trap. Roof spikes placed on a small surface can be effective if you're creating a situation in which stepping on that roof is likely. One variation I've seen is to build a stairwell leading up with a launch-pad underneath. At the top of the stairwell (and right under the launch pad) is a flat panel. On the underside of the flat panel, are roof spikes. An unwary victim that steps onto the launch pad will find themselves launched up into the array of spikes.

A strategy I like is to hide underground in a basic bunker and build floor panels above you that players above can walk across. Place traps inside the underground area and select the panels for editing. Then you wait. That's a disadvantage of many of these trap approaches: they can require significant patience. When a player is walking across, you remove the panels from under their feet, causing them to fall directly onto the trap. Since you're in there with them, you can then quickly move in to finish them off if necessary. One of the fun pluses of this method over some of the others is it gives you a greater degree of control. You're not completely waiting for the other players: you spring the trap yourself. This gives you agency and, frankly, is fun.

Another method, this one arguably mean-spirited, is to build a trap around an enemy. This requires strong building skills, but if pulled off can put your opponent in a situation in which they literally have no options. The basic version of this is to surround your opponent with four walls and then place a trap on top of them.

Farming Pro-Tips

We briefly covered the process of mining or farming building materials earlier, but it's a point worth revisiting. Players, especially beginning ones, tend to waste unnecessary time gathering supplies, when a few simple tips would make the process go more smoothly. If you're ever wondering how other players seem to build up their supply stashes so quickly, here are a few pointers.

One important method to more efficiently break down materials is to look for the weak point indicator. When players don't know this is there, they may smash away randomly trying to break down objects into supplies, making unnecessarily slow progress. The weak point indicator appears as a blue circle on your target which shows you where to strike with your pickaxe for maximum damage.

Even once you understand the meaning of the weak point indicator, if you have a proper approach, you can further refine your farming process to maximize efficiency. The most time-conscious approach to farming is to move your character as close to the object you're going to break up as possible. Walk quickly up until the object itself blocks further progress: if it's a wall, we're talking about the point where you basically bounce off the wall because it's holding you back. Get to this point of maximum closeness and then stop. Center on the object and begin your attack. If your character doesn't move, the blue dot will stay in the same spot, right in front of you, and you can just hit it repeatedly with your pickaxe until it gives way.

Be sure to gather as much as you can while you have the chance. If, late in the game, the storm forces you to abandon your base and you have to build another, you might have few options for gathering more material. Better to work from a surplus.

Chapter 4
Ramps and Stairs

Ramps and Stairs

Stairs are a very commonly built structure in **Fortnite**. We've already discussed them a bit but we will get into more detail here. I'll talk about the different types of stairs designs and will also talk about pyramid slopes or ramps, a less popular option but one with a few advantages.

The most basic purpose of stairs is to give your character access to higher areas that would normally be out of your reach. In the most basic default design, stairs appear as rickety-looking boards laid across planks.

This looks like ramps, and are often referred to as ramps by players. If you build in brick or metal, they actually more resemble the actual stairs, and of course prove less vulnerable to enemy destruction. You lay stairs down section by section. By building in this way, you can create a stairway to take you up the side of the mountain, atop a structure such as an enemy base, or if you want, just up. Remember, the height advantage is over overriding strategic importance when engaged in combat, and stairs are one of your major tools available to help you achieve this goal. As you're building, you can rotate stairs by pressing the R key or reversing your mouse to mirror their placement. Stairs are also necessary to reach treasure hidden away in attics and can provide you with some cover, although in that respect they are not as effective as a wall.

On a case-by-case basis and depending on the situation, you might want to get a little more out of your stairs. There are several options to build with a strategic purpose. Access the editing feature to choose from among the different available stair designs. Remember that you need to be on even ground in order to edit stairs. Once in editing mode, you will have access to different stair types beyond the basic one described above.

You can create narrow angled stairs in which the direction of the stairs changes between sections with a small landing in between. These can be used for multiple creative uses including getting access to higher ground in cramped locations. They also can be less obvious than the basic stairs, thus leaving you less open to detection from a distance and ultimately attack.

Another option is spiral stairs, which also can prove situationally quite useful. Spiral stairs reverse upon themselves at a severe angle, reversing directions between sections. This further narrows your build footprint, creating stairs that take up less space in all directions except altitude. Travel will be less direct, but you'll be less open to attack, often a reasonable tradeoff. These can be good to include in forts and can also prove useful in building around obstacles.

You can also make narrower stairs (half the width of the standard build unit) with railings. These can prove useful for gaining access in cramped locations and the side rails provide you with a barrier to protect you from accidentally falling, which can be a danger in tight areas.

When you enter the editing mode after placing a section of stairs, you will see a flat three by three grid of blue semi-transparent boxes with the center tile missing. Along the sides, two of the boxes have arrows. By grabbing and dragging the corner boxes from the grid, you can decide what kind of stairs to place. Grabbing one of the corner boxes and dragging it in one direction to the nearest corner will give you one of the narrower staircases, half the standard width and with a railing. Dragging it to the next corner after that will give you an angled staircase and dragging it to the third corner will give you the spiral staircase configuration. Clicking across the center boxes will allow you to return to the default arrangement.

Another option, favored by some, is pyramid ramps. These are very similar to the standard ramps and stairs. Although they look slightly different, they function practically identically. They arguably have slight advantages of being faster to place and quicker to edit.

Ramp Rushing

One common tactic among skilled and experienced players is ramp rushing. This refers to aggressively building a sequence of ramps from which to get the drop on enemies and quickly dispatch of them. Ramp rushing can be an effective tactic, really one of the only effective ways to reclaim the high ground in certain situations, but it can also be frustrating to deal with. As I said, this is an aggressive technique, and it's difficult to counter with merely returned aggression.

In this section, I'll talk about both: how to ramp rush to give yourself the advantage and how to deal with it when an opponent manages to ramp rush themselves to the high ground advantage over you.

To effectively execute a ramp rush, run forward while moving in a circular pattern. You'll be building constantly as you proceed ahead. You're going to be building walls supporting stairs as you build and climb. There is definitely a rhythm to this, which you can improve upon and master with practice. The gist of it is this: build your stairs when your character is at the uppermost point of the circle, and drop in your walls at the bottommost point. If you do this, your stairs will be over the walls which provide them with support and protection from attack. If your timing is off, there's the possibility you might drop a wall *on top* of the ramp you are climbing. Obviously, this is not optimal and could make the difference between success and failure in a heated combat, possibly with another aggressive ramp rusher. Like I said, you'll get the rhythm with a little practice, and it's a technique worth learning.

It's important to time your ramp rush properly. If you see an opponent in the distance, try to damage them using one of the long-range weapons. A good technique by which to approach them is to run while laterally dropping ramps in front of you. Basically, you're moving back and forth as you approach and are always behind a ramp, this giving yourself cover as you approach. Once you are close enough that you can bring yourself in above them through a series of ramps, start building up, using the circular motion I described above. If your opponent is not particularly aggressive, or inexperienced, they will be at a bit of a loss to counter this. Speed and maintaining an aggressive momentum is key in this situation. A more passive opponent may be easy to take out by this method. A more aggressive one might try to counter you with a ramp rush in your direction. In that case, one opponent may become hemmed in by the other's ramp.

If all goes well, you'll have the high ground advantage and be in a good spot for taking aim and shooting down at your opponent, hopefully finishing them off. If you find yourself under your opponent's build, a good counter-strategy is what gamers have begun calling "turtling." Turtling is when you hide inside or under your enemy's structure. It's important to stay calm in this step. Basically, you've lost the aggression vs. aggression contest, and further aggression isn't going to pay off. The other guy has the height advantage, and if you reveal yourself, you're just going to get killed. If you hide underneath the structure he's frantically been building and wait for him to come looking for you, then you can jump out and quickly attack and kill him. This turns the tables, forcing your enemy to give up his height advantage when he goes down to ground level looking for you. It plays off the impatient attitudes that often accompany ramp rushing. Your enemy is in an aggressive and hectic mindset and when you disappear he feels compelled to try to find you and finish you off. If you can keep a calm head and remain behind cover until he shows himself, you can retake the advantage and defeat him. To really pull this off well, it helps to be able to quickly edit and then quickly switch to your weapons. Then you can lay in wait behind a wall, then add an opening when your enemy is approaching from which you can shoot them before they can figure out how to react.

A similar approach you can use when you are being rushed by an aggressive player is to build up, lay down floor panels, then quickly edit out an opening in the floor panels from which to attack. These are advanced techniques that rely on a combination of skills that you can build through practice: combat, building, and editing. Each of those three components can be important in an on-the-fly combat experience, and none should be overlooked. Think of it this way: you want to have a full toolbox of techniques. If your opponent is a strong aggressive builder, but not much for editing on the fly, your mastery of that technique could be just the competitive edge you need to

Another useful technique when dealing with a ramp rusher is to use the right camera angle and fight over your right shoulder. This will give you a slight advantage because the game is designed with a slight tilt towards the left that you can exploit. This approach gives you the better angle and leads to a slight advantage in combat. Many opponents will rush you more or less head-on, trying to seek cover as they go. You can keep throwing up and hiding behind ramps, but as you peek out from behind cover, do it from the right side. In many cases, this will put you on his unprotected left side.

Chapter 5
Base Attack Strategies and Weapon Review

Attacking bases is of the places where all of your previous experiences come into play. This can be one of the crucial interactions between you and other characters, especially as the storm is closing in and the game is nearing its end. It's a tactical head-to-head, and it is here that you need skill, strategy, and any intel that you have. It all comes into play: the strategies you've learned, the skills you've honed through repetition, the tips and tricks you've picked up. We've talked about running ramps a bit, and that's part of it, but if you see an enemy base in the distance, how you react and what steps you take can determine the difference between victory and defeat. Here's a place where players benefit from an array of different tools and strategies to be used selectively, that toolbox that I've referred to previously.

A good Fortnite strategist can mentally flip through their different options and think on the fly as they're approaching an enemy camp. You have to, right? Because, as we've established, your enemy is not 100% predictable. You can anticipate that you think they *might* do. You can bait them and hope they take the bait. But you just don't know. They might surprise you because they're thinking ten steps ahead, or they might surprise you because they have no idea what they're doing. But in any case, they can surprise you. So you need to be smart and flexible in your approach as you're coming up on a base. You also need to be alert and strive for a functional balance of caution and aggression. A modicum of caution will keep you alive, but when it comes down to it, a certain amount of aggression wins the game.

So, let's talk through a few scenarios of base attacking and the different decisions you can make depending on what you encounter. Let's say you see an enemy base from a distance. Already, there are multiple things you can consider. If you are in a good position (maybe looking down from a hill) and have a good long-range weapon, you might consider using it to weaken your opponent and making a ramp rush on the base. As we discussed in the previous chapter, you can run, dropping sections of ramps in front of you for protection as you move. A weakened foe is a good place to start with ramp rushing—it helps level the playing field advantage they have that comes from having the high ground. Take as much damage as you can from sniping, but then quickly move in. Once he is weak it's important to immediately take the offensive. Get in quickly, throwing up ramps in front of you. A series of lateral moves that push you forward. If he's using rockets, don't build up too quickly. You don't want to take damage in a fall. You'll need to be smart. This is the case with many of the scenarios we can anticipate, but in the moment, you need to actually be thinking.

It's never so simple that you can entirely go through a script of prescribed moves. The world of Fortnite is complex, with a nearly countless list of possible factors to consider. You need to be mentally agile and ready to adjust your approach according to what's in front of you. Sticking to your plan in the face of information that runs counter to it is the most foolish thing you can do. Flexibility, creativity, and mental agility will help you survive and ultimately help you secure a win. Consider that a little pep talk: just be keep thinking, keep reacting. Be sharp. Strive to find that tenuous balance between caution and aggression as you move in. You need to keep your momentum. Keep pushing him, keep pushing whatever advantage you have, but also keep yourself from taking any damage to the greatest degree possible. Too much timidity is a losing strategy, but a thoughtless aggression will get you eliminated from the competition just as quickly.

If he's going after you with rockets as you're on the march, it can make it difficult to build straight up. Anything you build he can knock right out from under you. Back down strategically as the situation calls for it then resume moving forward.

As you approach the base, built floors above you to cover your top. Basically, you're throwing up a wall with an attached floor above you. This will keep him being able to easily kill you by shooting straight down at you. If he tries, his attacks will destroy your protective floors, but at that point, you only need to throw up another one to maintain your cover. Being a quick builder can come in very handy in situations like this.

As you move in closer and closer to the base of his structure, it's actually easier to protect yourself. You reach a point where the angles don't favor his attacks, and if he tries to use something explosive on you it will have the effect of taking out his own base. If you get inside his base, do your own building. Don't consider that just because you're in your enemy's structure you can't add to it. One of the beauties of Fortnite is the flexibility of the building tool. Within his base, you can chop out the ceiling above you with your pickaxe and start building up. Build your own ramps, destroying his work and replacing it with your own. Extend your own ramps from within his structure until you can regain that all-important height advantage and shoot down on him.

This describes one possible scenario. Let's consider another. We'll rewind to the point where you first spy the enemy encampment. You might try to cagily approach, trying to get close without being noticed. Of course, this would be in a case where you're pretty sure you've not already been seen. The sound you're making as you approach is always a concern. There comes a point where you're close enough to be heard, but at that point, you can rush an attack. If you see that your opponent is actually building, this type of strategy could be optimal. He might be so occupied with building that he's not keeping a close eye on all approach vectors.

If this method seems to fit, you'll want to approach, cautious and subtle, taking advantage of all natural cover you can find until you're close enough to be heard. Then you'll make your move. What that move is depends somewhat on what materials you have available. A rush in which you attempt to build up in a massive push against your opponent is always an option, but if they've built high already it might be hard to overcome this inherent advantage that they already have over you. If your opponent is at full strength, this can be a foolhardy strategy. Also, remember that building makes a lot of noise, so wait until you're ready to commit 100% to this strategy. Once you start, other competitors *will* know you are there.

If you've made it until you're pretty close to their base, an attack on the foundation might be smart. If they've built up high enough, and you work fast, you can knock the tower down from underneath them and possibly kill them instantly. Even if they survive, they're going to be weakened and possibly a little disoriented. You might be able to easily move in and finish them off.

If you have explosives, you can throw bombs at the base, starting before you're even that close. I do recommend continuing to move forward because often getting in *really* close can create a slight advantage for you. Depending on the shape of the structure and your enemy's placement, moving closer to the base can effectively shield you from an attack from above. If you're doing a bomb attack, keep lobbing them at the base until it is weakened to the point that it disintegrated and the tower starts to crumble. If your opponent was caught unawares and was still hanging out near or at the top, and the tower was tall enough to begin with, the collapse of the structure might kill him. In any case, he'll be weakened and you can quickly move in with whatever weapon you have in your arsenal that is best-suited to a close-range kill. We'll talk about weapons later in this chapter and I'll give you some suggestions along those lines.

If you don't have explosives or another suitable weapon, a pickaxe attack on the foundations of a base can be very effective. Obviously, you'll want to move quickly, going from wall to wall and smashing them in. It may take a bit longer, but the effect will be the same, bringing down the tower.

Now, all of this assumes that your opponent doesn't act quickly and attempt to stop you. The unknown factor is always your opponent. You never know what they'll do, and you have to be prepared with a flexible strategy that can adjust as you gain more information. A quick-thinking opponent might get down to the ground level to try to take you out. This obviously puts you in a threatened position, but think of it this way: he's willingly given up his height advantage. That's why attacking the base can be so effective: you're giving your enemy two bad options to choose from. Stay up high and die when the tower falls, or come to the ground and give up his height advantage. A smart enemy will take the second option because in that route there is at least a chance of victory, but if *you're* smart, you'll be prepared for this eventuality and ready to execute a slightly different strategy if this happens and go on the attack. Remember too, you can always switch to building to give yourself extra cover, even if you're in the middle of destroying his base.

Fluidity between the different modes of play is a useful skill and one that you will improve with time. Although this manual is mostly concerned with strategy, the other important component, which I've alluded to multiple times, is pure skill. All skill, even skill in executing strategy, comes with time and practice. This will come. The importance of learning strategies is that this ascertains that you will be building the right skills as you practice. If you don't take advantage of all of the options Fortnite gives you and just love to frontally attack, you might develop some truly impressive skills at frontally attacking, but you probably won't win the game very frequently when playing against opponents who have bothered to build their skills across a variety of different strategic areas.

In the encounter I've described above—where you're attacked while within the enemy's structure as you're attempting to take it down—your choice of weapon might be important. Of course, your weapon choices are limited to what you've happened to procure along the way, randomly placed ones, weapons that were part of weapons caches, those you've taken off defeated enemies. But within what weapons you happen to have, it is important to know what situations they are best suited for. At this point, I will review the basics of the available weapons and give some suggestions for how they might be employed in the game, focusing not just on attacking bases, but also how they might be used in the other varied encounters that can occur during a typical gameplay session.

Weapons

Weapons are a crucially important element in Fortnite. While we've expended a lot of verbiages extolling the virtues of skills and strategies, superior firepower, when wielded competently, can determine the outcome of a battle. Weapons can give a clear advantage, and that is why players generally scramble to gather the best ones they can find as soon as they first glide to ground level at the start of the game and continually search for better firepower. Weapons are classified according to how common or rare they are in a color-coded system. When you encounter a weapon, it will glow in the color that represents its level of rarity. Moving towards less common weapons, the system is organized as follows: Common weapons are gray, Uncommon, are green, Rare are blue, Epic are purple, and Legendary are orange. Most types of weapons have something at the common, uncommon, and rare levels, but certain weapons only exist as epic or legendary. It just depends. There are many weapons available on Fortnite, and many variations, and at times new weapons and variations are introduced.

A good general rule for understanding the practical application of the rarity scale in terms of a weapon's use: damage tends to increase with rarity. If two people are armed with the same weapon, but one person has the common version and the other has the rare version, the person with the rare version will have the advantage, and if both players are equally matched for skill, it is likely the player with the rare variation will prevail. When you start looking at different gun *types*, that is to say, different style weapons as they are defined more broadly, the differences become more significant. When making comparisons across different gun types, what you want to look for to help determine the true advantage between the weapons, especially for relatively new players that might not have mastered the fine are of aiming, is the damage per second (DPS). This is determined by multiplying the firing rate with the damage score. Part of the equation is understanding your own strengths and limitations. If you are an accomplished shot, a gun with a lower rate of fire but a very high damage might be ideal. You could dispatch of an enemy with a few well-placed shots. If you're not very accurate, you might want a gun that scores well in terms of DPS. That way you can fire a lot of shots and thus increase your chances of making a hit, thus using your weapon choice to at least partially compensate for your lack of experience and marksmanship.

For example, there are assault rifles available at all levels of rarity. As they become rarer, they become slightly more optimal. That's not to say that someone with a common assault rifle *couldn't* defeat someone with a legendary assault rifle. Particularly if they had superior skill, this is quite conceivable. But if they do, they will be overcoming a distinct advantage. Think of it in terms of the high ground. It's an advantage, and although advantages stack the deck they can be overcome. In this hypothetical scenario, the unlucky player with the common rifle has a weapon that can do 30 damage, 165 damage per second, and has a reload rate of 2.3. Compare that to the Special Combat Assault Rifle (the legendary version). This weapon can do 36 damage, 198 damage per second, and has a reload rate of 2.1. The two rifles are evenly balanced in terms of their fire rate and magazine size, as these are the attributes that define them as assault rifles. As you can see, this imbalance gives a distinct advantage to the person with the better weapon, but it is not one that would be impossible to overcome.

So, what is the assault rifle good for? It can be a very effective weapon when you are interacting with opponents at a mid-range. These rifles can inflict some significant damage and are fairly accurate. The gun doesn't do as well at a longer range. The accuracy begins to diminish when it is used at longer ranges, particularly if you hold down rather than tapping the trigger. The spray of bullets begins to drift at these long ranges, making it more difficult to bring down an opponent. In short, this is not designed to be used as a sniper rifle. As with all of these weapons, there's nothing like hands-on experience for understanding their strengths and limitations. I'm giving you suggestions here, but once you've taken them for a test drive, you'll better understand. Try to use each weapon in the situation it is best designed for. Of course, sometimes you're limited by which weapons you were able to lay your hands on. In this case, do the best you can, but it is always best to understand what your chosen weapon is capable of.

Let's linger a moment on long-range sniper rifles. These are available in a number of different formulations for rarity and all into three major categories: bolt action, semi-automatic, and hunting rifles. None of these are common; they run the range from uncommon (one version of the hunting rifle) to legendary (a form of a semi-automatic sniper rifle). So, it is far from a foregone conclusion that you will find one of these prized long-range weapons in your game. If you are lucky enough to, it's important that you use it as it is intended. If you do, you'll find it gives you a distinct advantage over opponents.

These rifles are irreplaceably useful for eliminating targets at a distance. They present you with a scope interface in which you can exactly target the placement of your victim. These are tremendously useful when attacking bases. As in all other aspects of the game, there is skill involved, skill that can only be developed through experimentation and practice. You'll need to practice your aim and learn to factor in the slight drop that the bullet takes with great distance, as these virtual bullets obey the same laws of physics that real-life bullets do. Even though they have great forward momentum, the pull of gravity pulls them down as they cover great distances. Accomplished hunters and real-world snipers know to make allowances, aiming high when shooting from a distance. Over time, you'll learn how to make these adjustments based on how far out your enemy is in a given situation. Once you have mastered your aiming, you can potentially eliminate an opponent in a single head-shot before he even knows that he is being stalked, a great advantage on the field of battle. Sniper rifles are particularly useful in the final stages of the game, as the ever-shrinking circle of the safe zone forces players in closer and closer proximity. Altercations between players increase in frequency during this phase of the game. If you are lucky enough to be equipped with a sniper rifle, you'll be well positioned to hole up in a safe spot, behind some cover, and take out multiple enemies instantaneously without ever having to give up your location.

A fan-favorite weapon is the SCAR assault rifle. This is a truly versatile weapon, something that has endeared it to gamers. One of the great things about this gun is that, unlike the others highlighted in this discussion which really only have one or two situations in which they can ideally be employed, the SCAR assault rifle can be used in many different situations to great advantage.

Among it's selling points: The SCAR is very accurate. It inflicts significant damage on enemies. It's useful at any range: close, medium or long. Its selling points are not dramatic or in your face, but it is just generally useful in every situation. Truly a "jack of all trades," and for that reason, it is one of the most popular guns in the game. This weapon only shows up in Epic and Legendary versions, so it's a very uncommon gun. Count yourself lucky if you run across one.

Among sniper rifles, there is a bolt action version and a semi-automatic version. Both have advantages. The bolt action, even though more limited in a technical sense, encourages you to take your time and wait for the perfect shot. If you're using the semi-auto option you might be tempted to fire more wildly, spraying bullets rather than painstakingly zeroing in for the kill. The bolt action, by design, encourages best practices of a sniper rifle. Of course, either one of these long-range weapons is extremely advantageous and can give you a major edge over opponents at long ranges.

Fortnite has several types of shotguns available: tactical shotguns (common, uncommon, and rare); pump shotguns (uncommon and rare); and heavy shotguns (epic and legendary).

Shotguns are an integral tool to have in your armory. They are crucial to prevailing during altercations that happen at close-ranges. In any round of Fortnite, you can expect close-range combat to occur at some point.

Pump shotguns fire much more slowly than tactical shotguns but can deliver tremendous damage, inflicting as much as 95 points. One well-placed shot is almost enough to kill a perfectly healthy opponent. A word of caution: since these guns do take longer to fire, missing can be very dangerous, especially since you'll be using the shotgun at close range. If you miss with the pump, your enemy is going to have a chance to shoot back. Be ready.

The trade-off with the tactical shotgun is that it delivers less damage, but can be fired at a much faster rate. This allows greater flexibility, giving you second chances if you miss with your first shot. With these guns a perfect aim is less important, freeing you up to move around while spraying your enemy with multiple blasts.

Also working best in close-range situations are the pistols. Fortnite provides many options when it comes to pistols, with them dropping in various forms and at various levels of rarity. They also inflict varying levels of damage, with the most pared down version, the common pistol, only inflicting 23 damage, while the Legendary version of the hand cannon inflicts a massive 78 points of damage. Pistols are best used up close. They aren't particularly accurate at mid-range and are effectively useless as a long range weapon.

One great weapon, when used towards certain specific ends, is the rocket launcher. Interestingly, the rocket launcher isn't that useful when it comes to a one-on-one encounter with an enemy. They do tremendous damage if you get in a lucky shot, and if you're team-playing it might be a practical move to fire a rocket into a crowd of your enemies, but one-on-one combat is simply not what a rocket launcher is designed for, even though we may have seen them misused in that way in more than one action movie. Rocket launchers are designed for destroying things. Big things. In the world of Fortnite, the logical use for a rocket launcher is to take down forts or to devastate the environment. Firing a few well-placed rockets into a fort can quickly bring it to the ground and your enemy with it. Rockets can also be used to eliminate cover leaving your opponents with no place to hide. One potential hitch to keep in mind with rockets is that the ammunition for them is relatively rare, so you'll want to acquire as many ammunition caches as you can get your hands on one.

Another gun of great utility when it comes to taking down buildings is the minigun. Based on its intimidating design, you might be tempted to pull it out during combat, but it isn't optimal for these situations because the bullets tend to be thrown out in a relatively big spread and it can be difficult to aim with anything approaching precision. These qualities are not necessarily disadvantages, however, when it is being employed to take down building and structures. You can use it to obliterate an enemy's cover, and if a few bullets strike them as well, all the better.

The boogie bomb is another fun weapon of major destructive power. When intelligently employed, a boogie bomb thrown into a cadre of enemies can tip the outcome of the fight to your advantage. Be careful with this one though, because its destructive power has quite a spread. You can cause damage to your own character if you throw imprecisely or don't get sufficiently far away from the blast before it explodes.

Another weapon worth trying out is the burst rifle. This one can fire a three shot burst which will give you an advantage over a traditional assault rifle, particularly if you are not that skilled a shot. With this gun, you can compensate for a less than spectacular aim by effectively increasing your rate of fire by unleashing a quick burst of three bullets each time you fire. Using this gun will keep you alive and give you a chance to better develop your aim as you use it. This gun is best employed at some distance from your opponent; if you try to use it up close, you might easily find yourself outmatched, especially in cases where you face an opponent who is using a weapon better designed for close-quarters combat, such as some variation on the shotgun.

The crossbow is a fun variation, functioning very similarly to the bolt-action sniper rifle. It has advantages and disadvantages uniquely its own. Its bolts are heavy so they fall more quickly over distance, something you will need to learn to compensate for as you use the crossbow. It also has an extremely low rate of fire. On the plus side, it has unlimited ammunition, is nearly completely silent to employ, and does a huge amount of damage. Give it a try. It can be fun to use.

Speaking of silent operation, one thing we haven't discussed are silencers. There are a few options in this area, the suppressed submachine gun, and the silenced handgun. There's an obvious advantage to being able to dispatch your enemies without an accompanying high-decibel burst to alert other nearby opponents to your location. Silenced weapons sidestep this problem, and if you proceed cautiously with them, you can still be relatively close and remain undetected. These guns can be well-employed strategically as a weapon of ambush. If you come upon two or more people involved in a firefight of their own and they haven't yet seen you, with a silenced gun you might be able to take them all out before they even realize a new person has entered the scene. As they're taking damage without distinctly hearing the source, they'll assume it's coming from one of the opponents that were already on their radar.

So, what should your strategy be towards weapon acquisition and usage as you play the game? For one thing, don't pass up any opportunities. Keep your eye open for weapons from the very beginning. As a bare minimum, you should try to equip yourself with at least a shotgun and some type of assault rifle as soon as you land. The opening minutes of the game are often a mad scramble by players for the weapons that are lying about and/or eliminating opponents to access the guns they just picked up. You need to be fast and thorough in these steps. A shotgun will give you a leg up in close quarters combat, and an assault rifle will get you through in mid to long range combat. So, first thing, strive to at least get these two.

Once you have acquired a suitable selection of weaponry, you should choose your gun based on the situation you find yourself in and the range at which you are engaging an enemy. For example, when entering a house, it's always a safe bet to switch to your shotgun. As you round corners and explore spaces, you never know exactly what you'll find, but you *do* know that it will be close. A shotgun will easily be in range of any enemy in a house and will deal major damage. A shotgun will give you a clear edge over an opponent armed with almost anything else while in a house. In an open space, an assault rifle will serve you much better. Make sure that, whatever situation you find yourself in, you are using the right weapon for the encounter.

In gameplay, every second counts, and a useful step towards maximizing your efficiency in switching between guns is to reorder the weapons in your inventory. Experienced players usually do this when they have the chance, so when any initial combat dies down, take a moment to take stock of what you grabbed and to move them around in your inventory to be optimally placed. You'll probably develop your own system for where the guns are placed relative to each other so you can go in with the same expectation for each game. Place guns that you'll naturally be switching between right beside each other, so you can get between them with the simple push of a button. For example, getting between an assault rifle and a shotgun. This is a switch that happens all the time, as combat moves from medium to close range. The player who is able to quickly switch between guns without fumbling will be more likely to survive in this situation. If you're still messing around with your rifle while the other guy has always switched to a shotgun, you're much more likely to get killed because he's going to be delivering much more significant damage to you than you are to him. So, consider these issues and place your guns accordingly.

I hope this primer on the many options Fortnite provides in terms of weaponry has been useful. The weapons list isn't set in stone: weapons can be added or modified as updates are released. Of course, there's no substitute for picking up a weapon and trying it out. Explore your own preferences and see what each option is really capable of. It is through this kind of creative trial and error that the very best Fortnite players develop their own unique strategies.

Chapter 6
Secrets

At the beginning of the book, I promised that although our primary focus was going to be on the developing and building of functional strategies of gameplay, we would also cover some intel. That's what this chapter is about. Intel: privileged information that can give you a significant advantage over your opponents if you avail yourself of it. Much of this intel has to do with the locations of secret or hidden items, particularly chests and legendary drops. A good strategic move is to aim for these little know caches when you first jump into the game so you can get to them before anyone else stumbles upon them and then proceed to nearby buildings or habitable areas to take out combatants already engaged in firefights and relieve them of their loot.

Bear with me: I'm going to be jumping around on the map as we explore these different options. At times, I'll make suggestions for where to go after attacking the secret chest location, but as a generally valid point of strategy, if you've just landed and gone straight to one of these secret stashes, it is a good idea to then go to the nearest hotspot—and there are plenty of them. Hopefully, you've had a little time by yourself gathering loot and then you can sweep into an area where players have already begun going after each other. You can take advantage of this carnage by finishing off already weakened characters. Often, if you get there after several rounds of combat among players, you can finish off a possibly-wounded single player who might already have in his possession the treasure he gathered himself and that he collected as spoils of war off the other players that he has already defeated. In this way, taking a little detour to a little-known stash that is not being picked over by competitors can be a very smart strategy. It'll keep you out of unwanted combat before you're armed and will place you to capitalize on the aftermath of game-opening carnage without having to put yourself at risk.

On the northernmost coast of the island, almost centered on the east/west axis, just north of Anarchy Acres, is a hidden chest that is built into the side of a cliff. You can aim for this as you glide in. The chest boarded up into a little cubby hole built into the cliff. You can take this out with a few swings of your pickaxe and then help yourself to the treasure. From here you can go on to raid the nearby farmhouse as it is likely to have a few people already busy looting and fighting. You can finish off anyone so engaged and then help yourself to whatever they've found and checked the house out thoroughly for anything that they might not have found.

In the town of Greasy Grove, in the southwest corner of the map, there is a secret stash inside the large, blacktopped building that's caddy-cornered across the street from the burger joint. Land on that roof and then grab anything that's visible on the roof before going on to the extract the secret cache. You can then use your pickaxe to cut your way into the building (alternately, you can come in through the front door and up the stairs, but you might miss some guns on top of the building if you take that approach). The stash is in a secret room behind the wall with the kayak hanging on it. Smash away at that wall until it gives way and then you can go into this little room and grab the treasure. For even faster access through the roof, you can land on the smaller square that just out at the back of the building (the side opposite the burger joint) if you hack straight down from there you'll drop directly into the secret room. Be prepared for firefights after extracting this particular treasure because although this location isn't known to all players, Greasy Grove is a popular spot and other players are sure to be wandering about and it's likely you'll be heard as you go about your business. Right around the corner from the kayak room is a little inset area which players often miss that can have a couple of treasure chests in it.

On the northeast sector of the map, just to the north of the tip of the Wailing Woods, is an often overlooked chest below a large tree that partially blocks it from view. This one is often missed because player's paths don't often lead them through here. There are a few nearby houses, but it is easy to bypass this chest on your way to them. It's in the center of a circle of chairs. In one of the chairs sits a teddy bear, and across the circle from him is a scarecrow on a stick driven into the ground. It's either a cute or eerie scene depending on your point of view and how your imagination works, but the good news is that if you aim for this scene, the bear and the scarecrow are probably the only other parties you're going to encounter and you can help yourself to the chest. From there you can go to the houses to gather further supplies and take out anyone else who is already there. Don't overlook the abandoned ice cream truck. Although it's pretty small, it can spawn up to two chests. From here, to the south and west is a large willow tree that spawns treasures. This one is better known, but you might check it out as well in case it hasn't already been picked over.

In the most recent iteration of Fortnite: Battle Royale, one of the new locations that were added is the abandoned Risky Reels drive-in theatre, an area clogged with cars and overgrown with brush. Check out the cars, trucks, buildings and behind the movie screen for chests. You can easily find as many as six or seven here, so it should definitely prove worthwhile.

On the cliff outside of Anarchy Acres is a small meteorite crater that is easily overlooked. You can find up to three chests spawned in this location, so it's worth a visit. You can also find antigravity crystals here as well. Some of the other meteor craters on the map were eventually filled in by the game administrators, so it's unclear how long this one will remain, but it's definitely worth checking out while you still can. Right next to the crater is a building that houses what looks like a TV set, complete with camera and what appears to be a sitcom living room. Look for chests in the studio. Be sure to check the rafters. Also check the trucks and garage outside: they can spawn chests as well. You can get a lot of bang for your buck in this area, as a fairly large number of chests tend to spawn considering what a relatively small space we're talking about.

There is another small crater, this one located near Snobby Shores, which is worth checking out. There you'll find multiple chests and meteorite shards that will give you an increased jump height. While you're in the area, the houses at Snobby Shores are always worth checking out, as they contain multiple stories and plenty of locations in which you can find chests. The area tends not to be overpopulated with players as some other sectors of the map so it's worth checking out. While you're there, there is a recently added building inset atop one of the mountains overlooking Snobby Shores. This seems to be designed to resemble the lair of a supervillain, perhaps one out of the James Bond franchise. There is a huge missile pointing from out of the top of the building, which resembles a skull in the arrangement of windows on its front. This building contains numerous locations for potential chest spawns and is definitely worth exploring.

Between Snobby Shores and Greasy Grove, there is a recently added element that should incite your imagination and probably hints at upcoming additions to the game in a future version. In this area, there is a decimated one-room house that has a dinosaur footprint right in the middle, splitting it in two. You can always find some chests here, so it's worth a look. As to what future plans by the game developers the dinosaur footprint alludes to, you'll have to wait and see. The meteor shower was the last big development, and it's easy to see this dino-footprint as foreshadowing something even bigger (literally).

In a valley to the north of Retail Row, heavily wooded with evergreens, there are a lot of places to find chests. There are abandoned big rig trucks, there are small circles of tents, and there are wooden watch-towers. Any one of these can contain a chest or multiple chests. People tend to overlook this as an initial landing location. From the sky, it doesn't look like much and probably doesn't seem worth messing with. All you can see is trees the trucks and towers might not look very promising. For this reason, you might be able to drop in initially without much company and be able to load up before you get into any major combat. Be alert though, because this location is close to multiple popular landing zones and you're likely to run across others fairly soon as they grab their initial stashes and begin to explore the island.

One good tip is to look for doghouses, usually located outside of farmhouses. Dog houses often spawn chests and the glow can be seen from the sky as you're dropping down. These can be found in various locations on the map, so consider this item on the list just a tip of something to be on the lookout for. Since they're easily spotted, they aren't, strictly speaking, secret, but if you have it in the back of your head that you're going to keep an eye out for loaded doghouses you might be the one to get there first. Along the same lines, you can break down the silos you find on farms to build up your materials stash and look for chests.

On the coast overlooking the ocean right on the edge of Lonely Lodge is a large mansion. There are elaborate stonework and lots of greenery in the front as you approach. In this building, you will find lots of chests from the very top, where there is a workout room, to the basement, which has a hidden room with a view of the ocean. Go from top to bottom (or bottom to top) collecting all of these chests and stashes.

On the east coast of the island, close to the top, north of Lonely Lodge and just to the east of Wailing Woods there is a hidden chest that is secreted away atop a big rig truck that is dramatically hanging precariously over the edge of a cliff overlooking the ocean. Proceed with caution because it is possible to send the truck plummeting down and yourself with it. Needless to say, your character will not survive the fall, as it is a very steep drop. So, carefully climb up on the truck to open the chest. If you choose, you may then break down the truck for materials, but if you choose to do so, be very careful and do it from a position of safety. This is a good location to choose for your initial drop. Since it's not well-known, you might be able to load up without facing much danger from other players, and since you're up there anyway, there are some sheds in the vicinity that you can loot as well.

There is a secret underground bunker beneath the unassuming blue house, the one with the lopsided windows and a vintage car parked out front, in Salty Springs. Go down the basement stairs. Under the stairs, you'll find a pile of boxes. Once you destroy these, you'll reveal *another* secret set of stairs leading further down. Once down there you'll find a secret control room with computers and monitors of unclear purpose arrayed in a semicircle around a couple of chairs. It looks like the secret hideout of a superhero or mad scientists. Like so much of Fortnite, the abandoned locations raise questions, and if you're imaginative you immediately begin concocting stories to go with them. In this secret lair, you'll find up to two chests. The house as a whole will probably have another two or three total that you can raid, so it's a worthwhile stop.

There is dilapidated looking farmhouse near Shifty Shafts. You'll recognize it by its fading and inconsistent blue-green paint and the unpainted wooden picket fence that practically surrounds it. This house has had a basement added that contains in it a small studio with a computer and a desk with a camera and microphone and green screens on all sides: basically, it seems designed to represent the studio space of an ambitious YouTuber, in an apparent nod to the fanbase of the game and the importance streamers have had to its popularity and as a voice for disseminating content and tips. Around this little mini YouTube studio, you can usually find multiple chest spawns. This location hasn't always been here and isn't that well known so it's worth checking out.

Down towards the southern part of the island, near the southeast corner of Fatal Fields, are a few great locations for hidden chests. One of them is located in the shadows of some very tall trees that have grown densely together. On the southwest part of the same town is another chest you can grab as you're moving on. It's located in a barn behind some haystacks and bales. This one isn't hard to find but is often overlooked nonetheless. There is another chest that you can usually find nearby at the top of a small rise in a little patch of dirt and another in a little inset cliff inside the quarry. This one is easy to miss and is often left untouched. You can grab any more available loot within the quarry proper, and then, as you're surrounded by rocks anyway, you're in a great position to start loading up on bricks to use in your later building. Don't spend too much time though. Your work will be loud, other players will be around, and it's always good to stay on the move and ahead of the storm.

There is a hidden chest at the racetrack to the east and slightly south of retail row. You can make out the racetrack on the map as a series of roads, and indeed, it is not the racetrack itself that is hidden. All but the newest players should be familiar with its location. But once you drop in, there is a little wooden structure, the one closest to the cliff, that features a set of wooden steps leading up to a raised patio with two large umbrellas that should be easily visible as you glide in. This structure usually spawns two treasure chests underneath that could be easily overlooked. On top of the platform, you'll often find as many as three randomly spawned caches of supplies as well. It adds up to making this unobtrusive little structure a good bet to load up at the start of the game. After you've cleared it out, you might head over to the nearby house, grabbing any spawns you pass along the way.

On the north side of town in Retail Row, there is a secret room that is often overlooked by players. This is a large grocery store. If you're on the corner facing the cliff, begin smashing with your pickaxe into the roof on the right-hand side. You can drop through the hole you make into the secret room. Then you'll want to go through the building, grabbing weapons and items that you'll find between the grocery shelves and clear it out of any competition as necessary. There are trucks parked behind the store and these often contain chests, so be sure to check them out while you're here. As Retail Row is a popular location, there is always a lot of activity, so work quickly and be prepared to fight if you need to. Don't let that guard down!

The above represents a pretty comprehensive list of some of the best little-known location to pick up chests and gain an early competitive advantage over other players. As I'm sure we've all experienced, the early phases of the game can really determine what happens later. If you fail to procure weapons and resources early, you can easily be eliminated by the first competitive player you encounter. One thing to bear in mind though: the world of Fortnite is not static. What is secret today may become common knowledge in time. The map is also ever-changing in a quite literal sense. As updates are released locations are added or deleted or modified. You never know when a new basement might appear with a wealth of previously unexpected riches. So, how can you, as a Fortnite player, use this information? Never stop exploring. I've updated you on some of the best locations I know of, places that tend to have good stashes that the average player doesn't know about, but I and other players only find these by exploring. Exploring may seem counter to a winning strategy. It can be. If you're exploring, you don't know what you will find. It could be a pleasant surprise that will give you a competitive edge and help you win the game, or it could leave you underequipped and outgunned as the storm closes in. Exploring is an important part of the game, but it is not a sure bet. Stick to the strategies that work for you, but every once in a while, take a risk. Put yourself out on a limb and explore a part of the island that is previously unknown to you. Maybe you'll find that super-secret stash that's *not* on my list.

Conclusion

Thank you for making it through to the end of *Fortnite: Become a Pro in Battle Royale with Secret Building, Combat Strategies, Hidden Chests, and More!* Let's hope it was informative and able to provide you with all of the tools you need to achieve your goals of becoming a true pro in the highly competitive world of Fortnite: Battle Royale.

The next step is to take these tools and strategies and incorporate them into your gameplay. As I stated up front, being a professional in terms of Fortnite means being a highly trained player. Basically, it's someone who takes his or her job seriously and is really good at it—someone who would be paid if it were a real-world occupation and not a game set in a virtual world for entertainment. As I also stated, being a Fortnite pro is analogous to being a soldier, perhaps a private soldier of fortune. The things you need in order to become a pro in this sense are strategies, intel, and skills. The bulk of this book was designed to give you strategies and to help give you the toolbox of concepts necessary to develop your own. The last chapter went into great depth with intel: secrets that beginning players may not know on their own. I laid these out for you to exploit to your own advantage when playing. The third element, skill, is up to you. Skill comes through practice. You should now be well-placed with a strong set of strategies and some effective and reliable intel, to begin practicing, already at a slight advantage over players who have not read this book. Every time you play Fortnite, you are practicing, but now that you have some foundational concepts and ideas, your practice can be more purposeful and directed. As you practice strategies, for weapons gathering, for building, for base building or ramp rushing, for approaching combat situations: you can master each one of them. A strategy, an approach that you understand conceptually based on my description, can become a skill that you can use to achieve victory on the field of battle. My hope is that if you've read this book you use it as a starting point from which to build up your skillset to achieve your own legendary status as a Fortnite master.

Finally, if you found this book useful in any way, a review on Amazon is always appreciated!

Book - II

Fortnite: Battle Royale

The Ultimate Guide to Improving Your Gunplay for Winning EVERY BATTLE ROYALE Like a PRO!

By

Pro Gamer Guide

Introduction

Congratulations and thank you for downloading *Fortnite: Battle Royale: The Ultimate Guide to Improve Your Gunplay for Winning EVERY BATTLE ROYALE Like a Pro.*

The following chapters are stuffed with pro-level tips to bring a new or average player to pro status in their gunplay. Learning how to fight and how to pick your weapons are just the beginning. Once you dive into the world of Fortnite, you will realize there is more than just luck to make sure you win Victory Royale each and every time you play. Browse these chapters to learn about basic gunfighting strategies and the ins and outs of the weapons you can encounter in the game. Once you have built the foundation of your gunplay knowledge, bring your gaming to the next level by learning how to customize your platform to get the best results. For example, if you always play on a computer, check out Chapter 3 to learn keybinding strategies and in-game adjustments to play like a pro.

Once you customize your platform, now you are ready to push past basic and get into the skills of a pro. Learn about topics like the bullet bloom and aiming strategies. Adapt your playstyle from Solo mode to Squad with ease.

So no matter if you are just starting out or ready to secure your pro status, use this manual for taking your gunplay to the next level and winning every game like a pro!

There are plenty of books on this subject on the market, so thanks again for choosing this one! Every effort was made to ensure it is full of as much useful information as possible, please enjoy!

Chapter 1
Basic Gunplay Tips for Improving the "Average" Player

Gunfighting Strategies for the "Average" Player

If you are new to the game or just have a few plays under your belt, you may consider yourself an "average" player. This means you may have won one Victory Royale or come close, but it is not because of strategy or skill. As you venture further into this guide, use the following tips to help you build a solid gunfighting strategy before adding on the more advanced techniques.

1. When you jump from the battle bus, you need to have a landing spot in mind. The more popular places mean more immediate battles. If you are still figuring out the weapons and fighting skills, you may or may not want to go there. It all depends on your goals. If you are going for distance in the game, stay away. If you want to practice engaging your enemy and a fast-paced fight, drop in. The more you practice fighting, the better you will be. Therefore, it is smart to head to places like Flush Factory and Tilted Towers.

2. Jot down where you find loot, especially chests. This way you know where to look next time! You may not always get that legendary weapon you found this time, but chances are high you will get something good if it shows up there again. And ALWAYS grab the ammo.

3. Stay up high, or get there as soon as possible, especially in a fight.

4. Attack your enemies with your weapon of choice, but keep in mind a backup weapon you can switch to if your first runs out of ammo. This way you do not have to wait for the reload while engaging. Those few seconds can cause you to lose the battle. If you cannot switch to a backup weapon, find cover to give yourself a chance.

5. Be bold; do not hesitate. When you are fighting, avoid giving your opponent the opportunity to recover. Start firing and keep firing, until you get them down.

Weapons to Choose from and Rarity Classifications

When you are about to land on the map, you have one thing in your inventory: your pickaxe. This tool is vital to your success but is not the best weapon for defending and attacking your enemies. This means, the moment you land, you need to be on the lookout for weapons to stock up on. And this search continues through the entirety of the game until you are standing victorious. In order to aid you in your quest for the best inventory of weapons, you need to understand the rarity of weapons and the different options to choose from. These weapons are also good in a variety of situations, so you need to know when to use them for the best results. The following section will outline your best recommendations from beginner to pro and all levels in between.

Rarity types

Grey- Common

Green- Uncommon

Blue- Rare

Purple- Epic

Orange- Legendary

A purple or orange weapon is harder to get ahold of in the game, but when you get one, hold on to it! These typically inflict the most damage and give you an advantage over your enemies. Also, always discard a grey version of a weapon in favor of another, rarer version. You will know immediately what rarity the weapon is when it is dropped because it glows the color.

Types of Weapons

There are 10 different types of weapons you can find in Fortnite Battle Royale, but the list is always changing with new updates occurring often. For example, a weapon may no longer be offered all together or the features of the weapon and rarity can be altered. Keep abreast of the changes because you may be searching for something that no longer exists or leave something behind you does not know what it does.

In general, the following options for weapons include:

- Assault rifle (AR)
- Shotgun
- Minigun
- Grenade
- SMG
- Sniper rifle
- Rocket Launcher
- Pistol
- Crossbow
- Grenade launcher

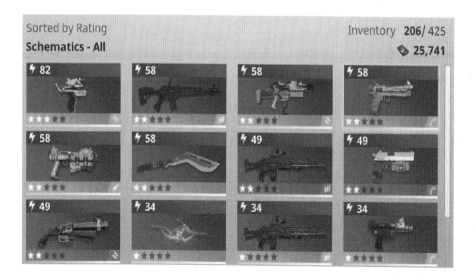

Assault Rifle

Rarity: Common, uncommon, rare

This is the most "common" weapon in the game. The common AR can deliver 165 damage in 1 second, with a full damage of

30, a firing rate of 5.5. The magazine holds 30 rounds and has a reload speed of 2.3 seconds.

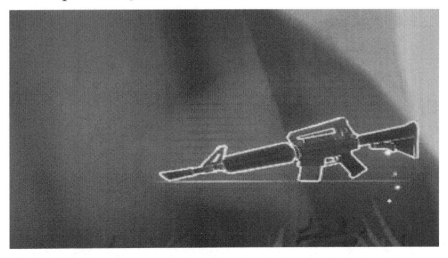

The rare version offers a slightly faster reload speed of 2.2 seconds and inflicts just slightly more damage at 33, but the damage per second is what makes it stand out. Compared to the 165 of the common AR, the rare AR offers 181.5, a significant advantage if you can get your hands on it.

Special Combat Assault Rifle

Rarity: Epic, Legendary

Similar in many ways to the regular assault rifle, the special combat AR offers a 30 clip magazine, reload of 2.2 or 2.1 seconds, and firing rate of 5.5. Again, the majority of the difference rests in the overall damage and damage per second for these weapons. The legendary special combat AR delivers 36 overall damage and 198 damage per second.

Burst Assault Rifle

Rarity: Common, Uncommon, Rare, Epic, Legendary

This is the weapon that comes in all rarities. It ranges from a reload speed of 2.9 to 2.3 seconds. This difference does not seem a lot on paper, but in the game, you will notice it. In addition, a legendary AR Burst can dole out 34 overall damage and 134 damage per second while its common rarity only delivers 109.7 damage per second and 27 damage overall. No matter the rarity of the weapon, an AR Burst has a magazine of 30 and a firing rate of 4.06.

Scoped Assault Rifle

Rarity: Rare, Epic

It can be said that this is one of the smaller weapons. While it may not be small in size, much of what the gun offers is "small." The damage, compared to other AR's, is less overall and per second. For example, the epic scoped rifle damage is 24, causing 84 damage per 1 second.

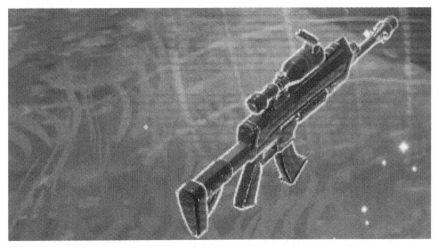

A major difference from a special combat or traditional AR. The firing rate is 3.5 and the magazine only holds 20 rounds, unlike the others in this category that hold 30.

SMG

Tactical SMG

Rarity: Uncommon, Rare, Epic

The deadliest weapon you can gather is the Tactical SMG. This is because it can dole out up to 234 damage in 1 second. It also has a firing rate of 13, no matter the rarity. The magazines also carry 35 loads, no matter the rarity. There is a slight difference between the overall damage and reload speed, but it is the damage per second that makes this weapon stand out from all the others, including the alternative choice, the Silenced SMG.

Silenced SMG

Rarity: Common, Uncommon, Rare

Another powerful weapon, offering damage per second for a rare version at 171, a silenced SMG is created to damage well with little noise. The reload speed is faster than the Tactical option, offering a reload speed for the common version at the same speed as the Epic Tactical version, which is 2.2 seconds.

The rare version has a reload speed of 2 seconds flat. The magazines are slightly smaller, holding only 30 rounds, and the firing rate is 9. The overall damage ranges from 17 to 19.

Pistols

Revolver

Rarity: Common, Uncommon, Rare

Inflicting an overall damage of 60 for the Rare version, this weapon is not the deadliest choice you will find on the map. It does inflict up to 54 damage per second; however, the reload rate is up to 2.4 seconds, the magazine only holds 6 shots, and the firing rate is less than 1. It is a good gun to grab if you must but otherwise, trade it out for something a bit more effective.

Pistol

Rarity: Common, Uncommon, Rare

While the overall damage a pistol can inflict is low, only delivering 25 damage for the rare version, the damage per second is impressive. The common pistol offers 155 damage per second. It also shares the highest firing rate in this category at 6.75. The magazine holds 16 and the reload rate is low, only 1.4 seconds for rare and 1.5 seconds for common.

Suppressed Pistol

Rarity: Epic, Legendary

Similar to the standard pistol, this gun has the same magazine size, a slightly faster reload rate at 1.3 seconds and a firing rate of 6.75. But that is where the similarities end. Getting your hands on this gun means you can inflict an overall damage of 26 or 28 and up to 189 damage per second.

Hand Cannon

Rarity: Epic, Legendary

It takes about 2 seconds to reload, only holds 7 rounds in a magazine, and has a firing rate of 0.8, but this gun is not something to dismiss. Inflict overall damage up to 78 for the legendary hand cannon, and up to 62.4 damage per second.

Shotguns

Pump Shotgun

Rarity: Uncommon, Rare

You can expect a long reload time with any shogun and this is no exception, but in terms of speed, it is the fastest in its class. You can reload the rare version of the pump shotgun, compared to the 6.3 seconds you will find in other versions. The magazine holds 5 rounds and has a firing rate of 0.7, but the overall damage is up to 95, and the damage per second is up to 66.65.

Tactical Shotgun

Rarity: Common, Uncommon, Rare

This shotgun is the one that takes the longest to reload, up to 6.3 seconds for the common version, but it can be worth the wait. Even the common version offers a heavy hit; 67 overall damage and 100 damage per second. The rare is even more powerful; overall damage of 74 and 111 damage per second, making this the most damaging shotgun per second in its class. It also has the largest magazine, holding 8 rounds, and the best firing rate, 1.5.

Heavy Shotgun

Rarity: Epic, Legendary

This is your middle-of-the-road option when it comes to shotguns. It is powerful and deadly, delivering 77 overall damage and 77 damage per second, but the firing rate is 1, the magazine holds 7 rounds, and the reload time is as low as 5.6.

Sniper Rifles

Bolt Action Sniper Rifle

Rarity: Rare, Epic, Legendary

This weapon will take time between reloads, up to 3 seconds, but the overall damage can be worth it, up to 116. The damage per second for the legendary version is 38.3, with a firing rate of 0.33. In addition, you can only fire one shot at a time because the magazine only holds 1 round. If you use it, you better make that 1 shot count.

Semi-automatic Sniper

Rarity: Epic, Legendary

Not as overall damaging at the bolt action, this weapon only offers overall damage up to 66; however, it has many other benefits to offset this. For example, the damage per second is up to 79, the reload speed is 2.3 for the legendary version, and both versions have a magazine that holds 10 rounds and a firing rate of 1.2.

Hunting Rifle

Rarity: Uncommon, Rare

Neither good nor bad, if you get one of the versions of this gun, you can get in some good shots and cause a lot of damage. The reload time is the fastest for a shotgun, as fast as 1.8 seconds, with an overall damage up to 90. The rare version also offers 72 damage per 1 second. The magazine only holds 1 round, like the bolt action, but the firing rate is 0.8 instead of 0.33.

Minigun

Rarity: Epic, Legendary

It can take up to 4.7 seconds to start, but it has a firing rate of 12. It does not inflict a lot of overall damage, up to 17, but the damage per second is extensive, up to 204. There is no magazine.

Light Machine Gun

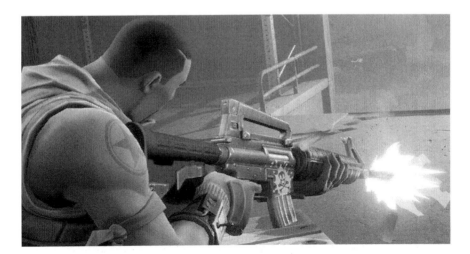

Rarity: Rare

A rapid-fire-type weapon, this gun offers the largest magazine in the game, with 100 rounds in 1. It takes 5 seconds to startup, but a lower firing rate (8) compared to the standard minigun. It also inflicts an overall damage of 25. The most impressive feature, besides the magazine size, is the damage per second. This is the most powerful weapon, delivering 200 damage per second to your opponent.

Rocket Launcher

Rarity: Rare, Epic, Legendary

It only takes up to 1.8 seconds to reload this powerful building-buster. The magazine only holds 1 shot and the firing rate is 0.75, but the overall damage is up to 121. The damage per second is up to 90.8. A pretty powerful punch!

Grenade Launcher

Rarity: Rare, Epic, Legendary

Another powerful weapon, this one takes a bit longer to reload, up to 2.9 seconds, but delivering an even overall damage and damage per second. For example, the legendary version delivers both at 110. The firing rate is 1 and it holds 6 rounds in 1 magazine.

Grenades

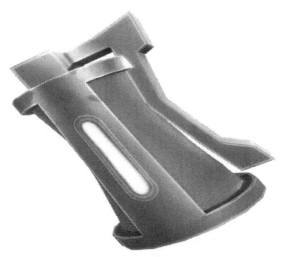

Rarity: N/A

These weapons are different than the guns you pick up. They inflict damage on buildings and people. One grenade hit can cause 50% critical damage and 393 structural damage. The damage per second is 210 and the overall damage is 105. There is a 5% critical chance.

Boogie Bomb

Rarity: N/A

It is as fun to watch as it is to deliver damage. Have fun making your enemies bust a move while they suffer 50% critical damage. Like a traditional grenade, it also has a 5% critical chance.

Impulse Grenade

Rarity: N/A

Another grenade that offers 50% critical damage and 5% critical chance.

Remote Explosives

Lay a trap for your enemies while staying out of harm's way. It delivers 70 overall damage and 800 structural damage.

Clinger

Rarity: N/A

While this grenade does not have critical damage, it still does hit hard. You can expect this weapon to inflict 200 damage to a structure and offer an overall damage of 105. It also inflicts 200 damage per second.

To Fight or Not to Fight

You do not need to jump into every engagement when you see an enemy. This is especially true when you are newer to the game. Instead, wait it out when you see your opponent. Make sure you can get the high ground above them, get your weapons lined up in inventory, and come up with a strategy to give yourself the advantage in the fight. If you cannot see a way to win the fight, swiftly move away from them to look for another chance.

However, you do not want to run from every fight. At times you will need to change the encounter, despite the setup and odds.

Not fighting may help you stay alive longer when you are new, but you will find that you have not gathered enough loot to survive the end game. You will also miss important opportunity to practice your gunplay skills. Instead, balance out patience and chance, learning how your engagement style can best suit your odds of winning the Victory Royale all the time like the pros.

Chapter 2
Tips Based on Your Platform-Gaming Console

Playing Fortnite Battle Royale is different depending on the platform you are using to play. And within the gaming console platforms, even playing on an Xbox One versus a PS4 can be a huge difference. Tweaking the sensitivity of your console can make a big difference and is a relatively simple process. The default settings are not good for winning, so it is worth the time to adjust. The adjustments listed in this chapter are not just about changing the in-game menus, but also help improve your aim and other essential functions. Unfortunately, adjusting your controls on a console is not as extensive as a PC, but some small adjustments can make a big difference. Find your console in the chapter and learn what all the buttons mean and how to adjust them for the best play advantage you can get.

Xbox One Keys

Functions	Key
Switch building material or Movement	L
Fix building/ Control camera	R
Map	+ - Up
Emoji	+ - Down
Go back to last craft item	LB
Set up trap or object	RT
Switch to another craft item	RB
Interact	X

Gather trap	Y
Switch to combat mode	B
Jump	A
View inventory	Double Rectangle
Open options menu	3 Lines

PS4 Keys

Functions	*Key*
Map	+ - Up
Emoji	+ - Down
Sprint or move	L
Fix building/ Control camera	R
Switch building material	L1
Move the item crafted	R1
Set up trap or object	R2
Interact	Square
Switch to another craft item	Triangle
Switch to combat mode	Circle
Jump	X
Inventory	TOUCH
Open options menu	O

In-game Control Settings

While there are not as many options for customizing the settings on a gaming console, the process to customize and improve your advantage is simple. The best customization is to open the settings menu and adjust the sensitivity option under controller options. Turn off the 60 FPS. It is defaulted to off because it makes the game visuals appear smoother overall. "FPS" stands for "Frames per Second." 60 FPS means that the game visuals are moving fast, at 60 frames per second. Turning this on allows you to have a better play instead of better visuals. Another change you can make in this screen is to adjust the Streamer mode. Toggling this setting allows you to turn off an in-game visual that can alert other players of your whereabouts.

While the Aim Assist is a frustrating element in the game, because it can seem like the game is choosing if your shots hit their target instead of your skilled aim, you should not turn it off in your settings. This will seriously impede your ability to play the game. As frustrating as it can seem with it on, it is worse when it's off. This means you need to get used to how the Aim Assist functions and prepare for its random selection.

Other adjustments are not restricted to just gaming consoles. Follow the guide below to help with your overall gaming strategy, no matter your platform:

- Choose Full-screen mode
- Adjust the resolution to 1920 X 1080
- Choose the default setting for 3D Resolution
- Set View Distance at least at Medium
- Toggle off Shadows to minimize distractions
- Set Anti-Aliasing at least to Medium
- Set Textures to Low or Medium only
- Set Effects to Low
- Choose Low for Post-processing
- Turn off VSync, it unnecessary
- Turn off Motion Blur, it improves efficiency

- Turn off Show Grass to help you see enemies easier
- Only turn on Show FPS if you want to track your performance.

When you are done making your adjustments, press "Apply" to save your changes.

Adjusting your PS4 Controller

Joystick sensitivity is incredibly important. The wrong settings can make playing unreal and chaotic. This is why adjusting the settings is so important to your success.

- Adjust your X and Y settings between 0.90 and 0.75 for the best results. It will drastically affect your shooting game.
- ADS Sensitivity for PS4 controllers is different than for PC users, but it does need to be adjusted for your down sights. Set this between 0.70 and 0.50.
- Finally, you need to adjust your scope. This needs to be more sensitive, so set is higher than the others, between 0.90 and 0.75.

You can also adjust your controller depending on what your role or intent is. For example, change some of your buttons to make it easier to build or fight. Ideal controller settings for combat mode are something like the following:

Function	Key
Aim down sights	L2
Switch to the last weapon	L1
Inventory	+ - Up

Emoji	+ - Down
Move	Left Toggle
Sprint	Double-Click Left Toggle
Confirm an attack	R2
Choose next weapon	R1
Pick up weapon	Triangle
Reload or interact	Square
Build or edit build	Circle
Jump	X
Aim	Right Toggle
Crouch	Tap Right Toggle Up
Repair	Hold Right Toggle Up

Another option is to adjust your settings to be more balanced between building and combat. To do this, consider changing L1 to Crouch and Triangle to Choose Next Weapon or Hold Triangle for Pick Up Weapon. Review the map by changing the + - Up to Map.

Adjusting these settings can make a dramatic impact on your game performance and overall gunplay. Keep in mind that there is still the bloom that you cannot eliminate, and other players will be skilled and making similar adjustments of their own, but it will greatly increase your gunfighting and overall play so you can win Victory Royale like a pro.

Switching Platforms from PC or Mobile to a Console

What you play on is both a matter of personal preference and availability. If you only have a phone or tablet, playing the mobile version is the only option available to you. However, if you have a tablet and an Xbox One, you can decide how you want to play the game. Recently, the ability to play against opponents that are playing on another platform than you have become available. For example, now a mobile player can challenge console and PC players, whereas prior to this update you could only play against other console players. This was because of the different play styles and functions available before, but the additional updates have helped level the playing field, although many still argue that playing mobile is still a disadvantage. There are some exceptions to this new update.

One of the hardest challenges of changing from one platform to another is learning the new body habits. This may sound ridiculous, but you learn how to navigate a keyboard and mouse or hand controls on your mobile, but those reactions you have practiced are not translatable to a console. Some find the transition easier, as there's only one controller and fewer keys, but others find it harder because it is more limited than the keybinds of a PC.

Some of the greatest challenges pros have identified regarding switching from a PC or Mobile to a Console are:

- No keybinds for the exact function
- Dealing with Aim Assist
- Working with 2 different controllers for play
- Screen clarity, not ad defined
- Building controls and methods are vastly different

The best advice when making a switch like this is to take time to practice. This may take a few weeks of consistently trying new settings on your controllers and in the game, as well as practicing building and gunfighting in the game, but it is important that you keep trying. Do not switch back and forth during this practice time, even if you are frustrated that you are a "potato" using a new system when you are a beast in the other platform. During this practice time, stick with the console and take the time and effort to learn. You will improve if you grind through this time!

With the new cross-platform play option, you will be coming up against others that are playing on PC or Mobile or another Console, and now even portable consoles, so having a better understanding of how a variety of platforms work can be an advantage.

A Note on Cross-Platform Gaming

Now when you are in the Lobby, you have a "Party Finder" option while before you would only be matched with players on the same platform as you or if you were part of a cross-platform party. But there are limitations to this matchmaking, and it all comes down to your platform still. If you are playing on a PC you will be able to play with and against players on a variety of platforms if they are in a cross-party; however, if you are playing in a Solo mode you will only be matched against other PC Solo players. No matter the platform you are on, when you select "Squad Fill" you will be matched with the player's on your platform as well. Some players have been vocal with the game's developers about not wanting to play with players on mobile devices or consoles, so now the "Fill" choice is no longer available for PC or MAC players that are part of a cross-platform party.

Creating your Epic Games account is critical to being able to play cross-platform with friends or in general. This is because all your information, including any purchased content, is stored in your account, along with your progress. It is important to note; however, that you will not see your leaderboards and stats cross-platforms with you. When you are going to play on different platforms, you must link your account to the platform you are using prior to starting the game. For example, if you normally play on the PC but are switching to a console, you need to link your Xbox One or PS4 to your Epic Games account so you can play in a cross-platform party with your friends. Typically, linking is only required for console and mobile players; MAC, PC, and Nintendo Switch all prompt for log in prior to the game, so it links it automatically.

To find your friends to play with, you need to create a cross-platform list of friends. This process differs from platform to platform. On a console you will manage your friends' list, adding or removing names, from the Main Menu. On Mobile, you will also be able to adjust your list. Using a PC, you can add or remove names to your list from either the Epic Games Launcher or directly through Fortnite's Main Menu.

Cross-platform on a PS4 requires you to link your PS Network account to your Epic Games account. You will then open the Options tab using your PS4 controller and scroll through until you find Epic Friends in the menu. Determine if you want your plays public or only viewable to your friends' list and determine which mode you want to play. Because you are considering cross-platform mode, you need to select either Squad or Duo. Once you select this, your friend playing on another platform can now join your team in your pre-game lobby.

To set up cross-platform on an Xbox One, you need to link your Xbox Live account to your Epic Games account. Open the Main Menu by selecting the Menu button on your controller and scrolling through the tab to find Epic Friends. As with PS4, you will need to select your privacy: Friends or Public, and your mode: Squad or Duo. Once you complete this step, your friends will be able to join you in the pre-game lobby. For your friends on other platforms to find you on Xbox One, you must be set to Friends or Public.

Those playing on a Nintendo Switch who want to play cross-platform, you need to link your Nintendo account to your Epic Games account. Press the + button on your controller to open the Main Menu and scroll until you find Epic Friends. Again, like the other consoles, you will need to choose Friends or Public for your privacy setting and Squad or Duo mode. Once you are complete your friends can then join you in your pre-game lobby.

The friends you are adding are people you already know, but you cannot find them with just their names. In order for you to find them in Epic Friends, you must already know their email address or their Epic account name.

A final note on cross-platform, those playing on an Xbox One cannot play against players on a PS4 and vice versa. Also, those on a Nintendo Switch cannot play against those on a PS4 and vice versa.

Chapter 3
Tips Based on Your Platform: PC

There are many pros that swear by PC functionality over any other platform. This is sometimes because of the customization options, but also because it is fast to build and fight once you learn your keybinds. Your keybinds will automatically be assigned when you first sign up to play the game, but you can change your options to anything that suits your play style. One pro's "secret" keybinds may not work for you, so try out a few of them listed here.

Customizing Your PC Mouse Settings

This is one of the most important adjustments you can make to both your overall game performance and your aim. This is not a simple toggle switch or slide bar to adjust, so it can take a new player a couple of tries and time to find the right level, but it is worth it. The default settings are not preferable for aiming because they are too high. You will notice some of the players do not know or do not bother to adjust their settings, so do not be one of them.

The adjustments you need to make are both in-game and out. This is especially true if you have a DPI Mouse with adjustable settings. This way you can really customize it to fit your play style. Some of the customizations include turning off the acceleration of your mouse, DPI's impact on your play, and determining the sensitivity settings that are good for you.

Mouse Acceleration Tuned Off

Prior to any other changes you will make, you need to first turn off your acceleration. Chances are if you have never altered your mouse settings before, this is not turned off. When it is on, your mouse will act differently as you move it across your screen. The feature is a system addition to help your mouse accuracy, but in the game, it actually is the opposite. Instead of your computer trying to predict where your pointer should go, you can take full control over the location it is placed and can rely on the movement. This means if you miss a shot because your cursor was in the wrong spot, you can no longer blame your computer.

Below are the steps to disable acceleration of your mouse:
1. Open your Window Search bar and type in "Mouse settings"
2. Click on "Change Mouse Settings"
3. Select "Additional Options"
4. De-select the box for "Enhance Pointer Precision"

How DPI Impacts Your Play

If you have a mouse set at 1,000 DPI it will move over 1,000 pixels per inch on your mouse pad. For shooting and fighting games like Fortnite Battle Royale, you need to adjust this setting to as high as 1,000 to as low as 400. If you go higher than 1,000 your precision will be severely impaired and will not be able to get clear headshots. Find your own setting level you like for this function, but most gamers put it somewhere between 400 and 550. You will need to decide if you want to move your mouse between shots or keep movements minimal. Larger arm movements when your DPI is lower means you can be more precise while higher settings mean you can make smaller gestures to get the same result. The larger hand movement to get more precise action is typically preferred, but you need to try it out to find what you like best.

For those that are unsure what their DPI is or if their mouse is capable of this, you most likely do not have a DPI mouse. You cannot adjust these settings if you are using a standard, supplied mouse with your PC. A DPI mouse is a gaming-specific mouse that you need to buy separately so you can alter these settings. It is worth purchasing if you play a lot.

In-game Settings for Sensitivity

In Fortnite, open the Settings Menu. Select the "Game" tab to open the options for sensitivity. Once in here, you need to adjust your settings as you see fit. The 3 main adjustments you need to consider are the sensitivity, the ADS sensitivity, and the Scope sensitivity. ADS refers to aiming down sights and Scope refers to when you are scoped in. The general sensitivity must be higher than the ADS and Scope. This alteration is important to allow you to pivot and face rivals easier and improve the accuracy of your aiming.

Suggestions for in-game sensitivity include:

- Adjusting mouse sensitivity, no higher than 0.5 and no lower than 0.3. The default is too high.
- For gunfights, adjust the sensitivity between 0.5 and 0.4. Setting it higher will seriously mess with your in-game experience.
- Whatever you set your ADS to, set your Scope slightly higher but lower than general sensitivity.

PC Settings

To begin, you need to update your GPU drivers and also your Window's version so it is the most current. Once you have done this, you can make adjustments to make the graphics clearer and actions more precise. The following instructions are for an NVIDIA GPU:

1. Inside "Control Panel" select "NVIDIA Interface."
2. Select "Manage 3D Settings."
3. Find the tab for "Program Settings" and locate "Fortnite." It may take a while to find it.
4. Set "Maximum Pre-Rendered Frames" to 1.
5. Set "Monitor Technology" to "G-Sync."
6. Set "Multi-display" or "Mixed GPU Acceleration" to "Single Display Performance" mode.
7. Set "Power Management" mode to the max.

8. Toggle off "Vertical Sync."

9. Toggle on "Threaded Optimization."

Setting Your Keybinds

When you begin playing Fortnite on a PC, the keyboard can seem overwhelming. There are so many keys to learn and master! This means many players do not take the time to learn the shortcuts and are wasting time trying to fight and build the hard way. There are the essential keys you will learn right away that can help you survive, build and fight, but then you need to rebind your keys to help you do it all more efficiently.

Below is a guide to help you learn the default keybinds and some suggestions on how to rebind for better play style:

PC Keybind Defaults

Keys	*Functions*
W,A,S,D	Up, down, left, right
Alt-Left/ Alt-Right	Cursor
Left Mouse Button	Fire, Resurrect
Right Mouse Button	ADS, change building material, reset edit, respawn
R	Reload
E	Use
T	Pick up, trap equipment
G	Edit building
F	Upgrade, repair
R	Building rotate
Shift Left	Sprint
1,2,3,4	Weapon locations
5,6,7	Ability locations

8,9	Gadget locations
F1, F2, F3, F4	Building supplies
F5	Traps location
Q	Quickbar switch
Down Mouse Wheel	Up slot, down slot
Enter	Chat
B	Quick chat, messaging
N	Pass note
Mid Mouse Button	Target spot
V	Select building material
M	Navigate map
I	Navigate inventory
Space	Skip Cut Scene
Left Ctrl	Crouch
Y	Push-to-talk

Keybind Tips

The following steps outline how you can rebind your keys to customize them to your preference:

1. Open Main Menu and select the triple-stripe icon in the upper right-hand corner.

2. Click on the cogwheel and select "Input."

3. Click on the key on your keyboard you want to change and then click on the new key you want to bind the action too.

Now that you know how to rebind your keyboard, you need to choose what you want to do. Below are some suggestions to consider when you customize your own PC:

For Building

Key	Function
E or Q	Building material #1, Wall
V or F	Building material #2, Platform

| V or F | Building material #3, Ramp |

For Building - Option 2

Key	Function
Z	Building material #1, Wall
X	Building material #2, Platform
C	Building material #3, Ramp

This second option can be a challenge because it is directly below your moving commands

For Building - Option 3

Key	Function
Mouse Button #4, Thumb	Building material #1, Wall
Mouse Button #2, Thumb	Building material #2, Platform
Mouse Button #3, Thumb	Building material #3, Ramp

Choosing this third option can be hard to get used to but with practice, you may find it preferable. It is the fastest option for building.

An additional keybinding option for your mouse includes binding your pickaxe to your side or middle mouse button. This extra bind can save precious time and removes a lot opportunity for risk. You do not have to worry about pressing the wrong key in the heat of battle or looting.

For Gunplay

Key	Function
E	Use
Space	Jump
C	Crouch
1	Pickaxe
2	Weapon #1

3	Weapon #2
4	Weapon #3
Z	Weapon #4
X	Weapon #5
Q	Quickbar Switch
Mouse Button #4, Thumb	Building Material #1, Wall
Left Click, Scroll Side	Building Material #2, Platform
Mouse Button #3, Thumb	Building Material #3, Ramp
Right Click, Scroll Side	Building Material #4, Roof
5	Traps

For Gunplay- Option 2

Key	Function
E	Use
1	Weapon #1
2	Weapon #2
3	Weapon #3
4	Weapon #4
5	Ability #1
X	Ability #2
Moue Button, Thumb	Quickbar Switch
Q	Building Material #1, Wall
F	Building Material #2, Platform
V	Building Material #3, Ramp
F4	Building Material #4, Roof
F5	Traps

For Gunplay- Option 3

Key	Function
F	Use
Space	Jump
Control Left	Crouch
E	Weapon #1
Mouse Button #3	Weapon #2
Mouse Button #3	Weapon #3
C	Weapon #4

X	Ability #1
Z	Ability #2
NONE	Quickbar Switch
Q	Building Material #1, Wall
2	Building Material #2, Platform
1	Building Material #3, Ramp
F4	Building Material #4, Roof
T	Traps

How to Switch to PC from a Console or Mobile

When you choose to play cross-platform, you will be paired with players that are on all other platforms that have chosen to play with others. There are a few exceptions, like when you choose to play in Solo mode, but for the most part, you can play with anyone when on a PC.

Before you get started on a PC, it is necessary to download the Epic Games Launcher. Once you open it you will sign in with your Epic Games account. From there you can access your friends' list or add friends. You can also be added to a match. If you do not want to play cross-platform you must play in Solo mode.

Many pros will tell you that changing from a console or mobile to PC can be one of the hardest challenges you will face while playing Fortnite. This is because you will be going from a controlled and less diversified gaming controller to in and out of game sensitivities, keybinds, and more actions to remember. But once you master your keys, playing on your PC can be the best way to earn your "pro" status.

The adjustment period of this adjustment can take a few weeks, so make sure to play often on your PC and do not bounce back and forth between platforms until you have mastered the PC controls. Another suggestion from the pros to make switching to a PC easier is to keep trying out keybinds until you find a solution that works for you. In addition, make sure to practice aiming, because you lose aim assist. That feature may have been something you lamented in console play, but when you are used to it for so long and then it goes away, it is hard to retrain yourself. Despite all these hardships, you can expect to make this change to improve the clarity of your game visuals and overall building strategy. Also, you will notice that the game loads faster.

All the challenge of switching platforms can seem unnerving and may scare you away from actually trying something new, but remember that the basic functions and goals of the game are the same, no matter what you play it on. Therefore, do not let it mess with your head. On a PC, you can expect to build more because you can react faster than console or mobile players. You can also expect to play Solo against more experienced gamers, not a lot of kids on consoles. Thankfully, your knowledge and experience will follow you from platform to platform. Even some of your stats! Do not hesitate to try this platform out and see how you can push your wins even higher.

Chapter 4
Tips Based on Your Platform-Mobile

Not very long ago Epic Games released a mobile version of Fortnite. This option allows you to play on the go, no matter where you are. But with a new platform comes new challenges. Some of these challenges include utilizing touchscreen controls and downgrading your screen size. To date, getting used to the touchscreen controls have been the hardest adjustments players have had to play on mobile. It completely alters the way you approach the game. To win on mobile, you must now anticipate other player's disadvantages, recognize you have new limits, and exploit the new functions you have access to.

To win Fortnite Battle Royale on your phone, try the following:

1. Playing Fortnite Battle Royale on your mobile is the same game you play on PC or a console. This is why cross-platform is allowed for mobile gamers. But just as any switch in platform requires re-learning controllers and keys, you need to practice with the new touchscreen joystick. Basically touching anywhere on the left of your screen will guide your avatar to do some sort of action. The right has a few buttons, too, including crouch, jump, and slow and quieter movements. A few buttons are

dedicated for fighting and aiming, while you can switch your menu view for building controls.

2. Adjust your sensitivity settings, especially for your camera. Wiping your finger across your screen moves your view around. It is important that you adjust the speed of this movement to match your play style. Consider adjusting your sensitivity to make your swipes shorter while keeping your move fast. Avoid moving too fast, as you can miss faraway players during a scan. There are 3 sensitivity settings you need to adjust for; general camera view, ADS, and scope.

3. Use headphones here, too. Just as with other platforms, being able to hear the cues in the game is essential. Nothing is different when you are playing mobile. Plug in so you can hear all the sounds of players and building and other important cues.

4. Become familiar with the new visuals and take advantage of them. These go along with the audio cues you will hear in your headphones. Unlike other platforms, the combination of the 2: audio and visual cues, you can use them together more effectively to sneak up on rivals and get the advantage.

5. Coving a lot of ground, picking up loot and taking out opponents is critical to succeed in the game. But on mobile, you are giving up visuals to control your avatar so you can miss important cues or items. To help with some of the limitations of mobile, Epic added a feature to

mobile that is not on PC or console platforms. This is the auto-run option. A quick double-tap on this button allows you to send your avatar running towards the direction they are facing.

6. Practice your building skills often and over and over again. Toggling to another menu to access build means many mobile players do not jump to build. This is a serious disadvantage that you can turn to your advantage on mobile. Learning how to build quickly on this platform means you can protect and fortify yourself for the win.

7. Even on PC or console, aiming a weapon is a challenge. When you are playing on an even smaller screen, you are facing an even harder challenge. Long range is especially hard, making all the missed shots more of a beacon to your location than to score you a kill. This means adjusting your play style. For example, instead of favoring an AR, consider opting for a shotgun or another close- to a mid-range weapon.

8. Use ADS when you are in a fight. This helps you tighten your view for a better shot. Instead of looking at the game from third-person, you have a view over the shoulder. This change also slows your movement down. The advantage in mobile is that you can fire rapidly to try to take down your opponent instead of relying on the precision of PC or a console. You can increase your

accuracy like you do on other platforms by crouching while shooting and staying still.

9. Enabling another new feature, "Tap to Search or Interact," is a good method for capitalizing on your advantage in mobile. Now in mobile you no longer have to switch to a "gathering" mode; now you can just run over it and it gets picked up. The problem with this is that you will pick up even things you do not need or want, meaning you will have to drop things constantly to free up space. Switching on "Tap to Search of Interact" means you have to spend more time grabbing weapons and loot, but it also means you will be able to filter what makes it into your inventory.

Currently, the compatible devices that can play Fortnite Mobile are all iOS devices; 6s, SE, Mini 4, Pro, Air 2, 2017, and all devices with iOS 11. It has been released that the iPhone 6 is not compatible with Fortnite at this time, but they are working on compatibility. There is talk about adding Android but it is not available for now.

To control your mobile play, it is important you become familiar with the following default settings:

- *Moving*- Left thumb drag on the touchscreen joystick towards the direction you want to move. Double tap to auto-run.

- *Aim and shoot*-1 finger drag across the screen to swivel the camera and tap quickly to fire your selected and loaded weapon.

- *Inventory*- 6 boxes on the bottom of your screen. 1 is dedicated to your pickaxe while the other 5 are set for your weapons. Tap on the item you want to use. Another method for accessing a larger view of your inventory is to click on the backpack icon on your screen.

- *Build*- Tap on the Combat or Build icon near the inventory icon.
    - *Select object*- a new inventory is displayed on the bottom of your screen. Tap on the item you want to use to build with.
    - *Select material*- In the building menu, tap on the icon for access to your wood, stone, or brick.
    - *Place and adjust*- The upper right-hand side of your screen has a button, "rotate," you can tap to move your build. "Edit" is on the left of the "rotate" button. Pressing it allows you to tap on the part of your build you want to edit or remove. To build an item, press "place" to construct what you want.

Adjusting Your Sensitivity Settings

Once you are in the game, you need to customize your settings. Below are some instructions on how to adjust your settings for optimal play:

Voice Chat

- Sign in or sign up for a Microsoft account
- Download the Xbox app. This is important because it allows users to talk to you from the other devices in party mode.
- Click to open the Xbox app and select the 3-people icon. This action begins a party.
- Scroll through your friends' list and add the ones you want in your party.
- Once you are done you can now chat in the game.

HUD Customization

- In the pre-game lobby, open the main menu
- Open the Settings menu located in the upper right-hand side of the screen.
- Click on "HUD Layout Tool."
- Within this screen, you have the option to select and move all the control buttons. You can put your buttons wherever you want on your screen.
- Within this screen, you can also adjust the size of the buttons and move around the build buttons, as well.
- To remove unused buttons, use your finger to swipe them to the edge of your screen and then off.

Switching from PC or Console to Mobile Platform

The process of changing from a PC or console to mobile play is a hard adjustment. You need to learn new controls, new cues, and new screen. But getting to this new platform is not any more complicated than other switches. For example, even on mobile, you need to have an Epic Game account that you will use to log in prior to playing on your mobile device. Once you are logged in, you need to add your friends and develop a cross-play party. Once you are ready to play and are in your lobby, the friends you have invited will be able to join you in your lobby as well.

While you can play cross-platform with mobile, you may still be at a disadvantage. This mainly had to do with the matchmaking system the game uses. Typically, the game tries to match like platforms together, and you will be placed in a hierarchy depending on your platform. This means PC player get the top, console next, and then mobile. If you have a cross-platform party and one of your players is on a PC, you will be matched with mainly PC players and rivals. The limited controls and visuals make you, as a mobile player, disadvantaged. Instead, create an all-mobile party to play to give yourself the best opportunity to practice and win.

When you are on mobile, after playing on a PC or console, you will notice that the graphics are different, some would say less advanced and audio cues are now visual instead. But the game is the same, including the ability to chat. Another interesting feature, that is attractive to players that cannot spend an hour or more playing the game, is that mobile matches tend to take less time, typically somewhere between 25 to 30 minutes. Part of this is because you can move across the map faster and it appears smaller on your mobile screen. In addition, as mentioned above, the gunplay in the game for mobile users is not as advanced as a PC or console user. This means the fights are not as precise or tactical.

Some of the common questions being asked about mobile, because it is still a new and beta feature include:

Q: Where do you request the mobile version of Fortnite?

A: Go to the game's website for the link: www.fortnite.com/mobile. From there you will be able to request to play.

Q: How do you keep up with the latest news and updates regarding the mobile version of the game?

A: Follow the game's blog and look for updates when they are released: www.fortnite.com/news/mobile-announce.

Q: Why do you have to get an invite before you can play the game?

A: The servers for the game need to be able to handle the player load. As they work to scale up, more invites are sent out. The purpose is to make sure the experience is positive with as few crashes or negatives features as possible. To be invited, you can either receive a friend's referral invite or you can sign up on the game's website.

Q: Why did a friend get their invite before you, even though you signed up before them?

A: If your friend got their invite it is because of several factors, including their iOS device, their location relative to a data center, and the order they signed up. If you know they got their invite, ask them to send you their "friend code" they probably received in the invite.

Q: Will the mobile version be open to you even if you do not get an invitation?

A: Eventually, in the future, Epic Games plans to offer Fortnite Battle Royale Mobile to everyone who wants to download and play the game. This means you do not need to request or receive an invitation to download. But this feature has not been identified yet because they want to be able to handle the number of players on the platform with minimal problems.

Q: Do you have to play cross-platform?

A: No, you will be playing against other mobile players unless you join a multi-platform squad. If you do this, then you will be playing against squads using multiple platforms. If you play solo or only with mobile squads, you will only face against other mobile players.

Q: What are some of the common challenges players are facing while playing mobile?

A: Some of the problems players have reported include lag time after landing and matchmaking crashes. These problems occurred early in the release and Epic has been working hard to overcome the issues of a new platform. If you have challenges while playing, try shutting down the game and re-opening it. Also, close down any background app's that may be running. Change from data to Wi-Fi or vice versa. If the problems continue to persist, you may need to shut off your phone and re-boot it completely. Other times, the problem is occurring at the game level and you will need to give it time to be resolved before playing again.

Crashing occurs most frequently on the iPhone 6s. This is probably because it is the oldest of the approved devices, but it should theoretically work well. Epic is trying to work around this, but it is most likely a hardware issue they cannot fix on their end. Newer iOS products are operating with a larger chip, which is part of the problem.

Another common problem appears to be the missing links. If you have downloaded the game but cannot log into your account or link your account, you are not alone. Epic is trying to resolve this problem as soon as possible, so you can choose to either be patient and wait it out until they have it fixed or you can go online to ask for help.

Chapter 5
Aiming and Accuracy Strategies

The easiest advice to give you from the pros is to practice, practice, practice. Get into as many fights as you can with as many weapons you can find, to figure out how they work best. Of course, that being said, it is wise to know some of their "quirks" before you dive in, so you can live long enough to learn from them. For example, did you know that if you crouch with certain weapons, your accuracy improves? But, on the other hand, if you crouch while shooting with another type of weapon, you expose yourself to headshots and more damage? All of this information you can learn in the game, hands-on, or you can keep reading to learn how you can improve your accuracy and aim before jumping from the battle bus.

Turning Luck into Skill

All weapons are not created equal, but they also do not perform equally in one situation, either. What this means is that the legendary weapons are generally more damaging than common or uncommon versions, but you do not want a whole bunch of legendary sniper rifles and no close or mid-range weapons. This means you may want to forgo grabbing another legendary weapon to make sure you hold on to the common shotgun. Ideally, you should stock your arsenal with 1 AR, 1 grenade, and

1 shotgun. You should be stockpiling as much ammo as possible, too. Of course, there are other items you are adding to your inventory, but for gunplay, this is what you generally want for your inventory.

"If You Build It...."

Building is almost as important as your weapon in a fight. It may seem silly to put away your weapon to throw up a wall or ramp, but you need to protect yourself from enemy fire while you are shooting at them, too. You can use the provided landscape, but if you do not have access to a rick or tree or building, having enough resources to erect even a basic structure can make all the difference in your success in the fight. Take every opportunity you get to fill your inventory with wood, brick, and stone.

Positioning is Key

Choose how you shoot at your enemy. As mentioned before, how you shoot is sometimes as important as what you are shooting with. If you find you keep getting dropped in a gunplay, consider how you position your avatar. Take the time to stop moving, crouch down, and aim your crosshairs at the other player. Many new players begin shooting from the hip, hoping a couple shots will hit the target. Just changing this up can make a difference. However; how you position yourself also depends on how you are engaged. If you are fighting in close range, crouching down while facing a shotgun means you just created the best target as your own head. This is critical.

Instead, stay standing and moving, hoping your opponent misses while you are landing yours.

Tap, Do Not Hold

For rapid-fire weapons, like a machine gun, only lightly click the button to fire one shot instead of holding it down to fire multiple. This allows you to have power and more precision. It also preserves your ammo for later fights. And when you tap the key, make sure to tap it slowly and with intention, not just holding it or rapidly tapping. It is about as much precision as possible, not spraying the opponent with bullets and hoping for them to hit something. That strategy will lose almost every time against a pro who takes their time to land a few good headshots on you. In close range, jump and move to make it harder for them to hit you before pausing to fire off a shot at them.

Target Practice

If your target is moving, either in front or behind you, try to predict where they will head next so you can aim their fire. This way they will walk into your bullet instead of you missing them as they move. If you are moving away from them, meaning you are trying to get away from the fight, do not try to shoot and run. That is a waste of ammo.

Instead, run, then pause to shoot, and then start running again. You only shoot and run if it is your only way out of the fight or you are avoiding the storm.

From a Distance

If you are fighting someone from a distance, you are going to be using a sniper most likely. When you fire a shot, take a beat before firing again. This is because your opponent will react quickly to your first shot but will probably resume their normal play when you do not engage again. They will think it is safe and make it somewhat easier for you to land another hit. Also, long-range gunplay means you almost will always be stopped and crouching, the best way to accurately hit an opponent.

Practice Sessions

"Practice makes perfect"

This is probably the most important tip you can be given to improving your gunplay. You can read and study all the components of weapons and fight but you need to get your hands on a weapon and try it out to understand what it can and cannot do. The more you practice, the better you will become at shooting and aiming, but it is also important to keep playing game after game so you increase your odds of getting a very rare weapon to practice with. Below are some of the additional strategies you can use to help you practice your gunplay to be able to enter any battle and win like a pro.

The Lobby

A relatively new concept (for Fortnite gamers, it may not seem that new now), you can now try out different weapons in the pre-game lobby, before boarding the battle bus. This option is amazing for you to get your hands on a weapon and try it out, learning the aim and firing quirks of the weapon. As you enter the lobby, look around to find different weapons on the ground. Pick one up and give it a shot. You cannot take the weapon with you on the battle bus, but at least you can become familiar with the weapon prior to having to use it on an opponent. This is a great time to try to get experience with rarer weapons, like a blue SMG. You do not have unlimited time in the lobby, but it is a good time to try it out with no risk.

Gun Practice

The lobby will not give you enough practice to really get used to firing a certain weapon. And there are some of the more common weapons you should be very used to using. This means you should spend time getting to know the ins and outs of the weapon and how it performs under pressure. For example, an AR fires differently than a shotgun. A machine gun fires multiple shots quickly but the precision is lacking. Learning how to control each weapon helps you learn how to use it under pressure in a fight.

Fast Practice

The best way to practice is to get into a fight right away. This means you should plan on dropping into more populated areas to loot and fight. This is a strategy for practicing gunfighting, not winning or surviving. If you do end up surviving after the initial rush, plan on moving away from the developed land to find higher ground and prepare for the incoming storm. While you go out, since you are in a practice mindset, try to engage in as many fights as possible, challenging yourself to try your different weapons and fighting strategies. Again, this is not about winning Victory Royale during this match; so do not shy away from a fight. You will lose, but as long as you walked away more knowledgeable on how to fight, you will have gained valuable skills to help you win the next time.

Mid-Game Practice

It is important that you learn the difference in fighting style in mid-game rather than just the early-game. Early-game, as indicated above, is a fast-paced race to get good loot and take out a few opponents along the way. But when the first circle begins to close in, and the center of the storm is getting smaller, your fighting style must change, too. This means you need to also practice getting into this part of the game and how to fight. In this instance, the drop from the battle bus should not put you in a populated area, but rather somewhere quieter. This way you do not rack up as many kills, but it will help you get to the mid-game more often than not. Once you make it to the first storm's movement, you will no longer be taking out opponents and gathering loot with no purpose. Now you are either racing to the center of the storm to take or build a high ground to shoot from or you are sticking to the edge of the storm to hide and attack panicked enemies. Get to this point and practice either situation. When you get good at hiding on the edges, challenge yourself to get into the middle and build up.

Hiding on the edges of the storm as it closes in allows you to use a cover for a little bit, but in the first couple storms, the damage the edge does can be repaired with potions. If you duck into the storm for a few seconds so an enemy loses sight of you or they do not see you in the first place, you can then attack them from the wall of the storm and take them out before coming out and healing yourself. Most of the time, players will be along the storm edge for 1 of 2 reasons: they are trying the same strategy as you are or they are new to the game and panic easily. Those that are new to the game will be easier targets as you play the edge. The others on the edge are more experienced, so engage wisely.

Taking the higher ground is a race against the others and time. Once you know the general location of the center of the eye, use the natural landscape and/or build up to be the highest player. This is a good strategy to practice when you have a good long-range weapon. If you find yourself with a good weapon and solid inventory of ammo, practice this strategy. It is also a chance to practice your building strategy. Practice hitting targets from above them and far away, and also keep opponents from destroying your structure. This is a more aggressive strategy for mid-game, so practice it to find out how you like it.

Late-Game Practice

It is also important to practice during the end-game as well. The strategy here is again different than other parts of the game.

The storm is moving faster and faster and there are fewer players, typically with more skill. Now is not the time to randomly spray bullets at others. Build up high and snipe your competition. When it comes down to the final 3, try to let the other 2 fight it out, and then take advantage of the probably weakened one to take them out for victory royale. When you see the final 2 fighting, get to a spot far away from where they cannot see you, and set up a shop to take out the winner. To get to this point, you need to play cautiously and with skill, but once you get to this point, practice being aggressive and keep engaging.

These strategies are not going to help your stats, but they will help you get much better at fighting. Do not fear being killed; you will lose more often than not doing this. But it will you get better and better in each encounter.

Know the Bloom

This is a common term you will encounter when discussing firing weapons in Fortnite: Battle Royale. The term "bloom" refers to the radius of the shot. To keep the game a little bit more challenging and open to all levels, Fortnite Battle Royale makes the bullets land inside a certain circumference related to the crosshairs of the weapon. This means if you keep completely still and fire several shots at your target with the same aim and target, the bullets will land in different places from one another.

Many people do not like this feature because they feel it impedes their ability to use skill to take out an opponent; however, Fortnite has yet to remedy this bloom for unpublished reasons. The reason they keep the bloom is irrelevant to your ability to fight more effectively. You need to focus on what you can control, and that is your accuracy of aiming and shooting. There is recoil after each shot, so you need to fire an aimed shot at the head, if possible. Then wait for the accuracy to return before firing the next shot. Expect, no matter how well aimed your shots are, only 40% of your shots will hit their target. This is great for new players who are relying on luck to hit the mark for them but frustrating for pros. Understanding there is a bloom and that you need to fire more shots to get a kill, you can attack with as much precision as you can manage. If you cannot get past this feature, consider relying on a long-range strategy as a sniper rifle can get the crosshairs on your target fairly well and hits can be deadly with just a few that land on the head. Shotguns are more scattered and better for close range, making accuracy harder.

Chapter 6
Solo Mode

The goal of Fortnite Battle Royale is to be the last participant standing. In solo play, this means you will have to beat out all the other players to stand victorious in Victory Royale. This is not an easy task, but having a strong gunplay game will help you get there more often than not. To help you win the game like a pro, you need to be smart about how you stock your inventory and how you attack your enemies. This approach is very different than if you were fighting with a friend in Duo or a group of friends in Squad mode.

Gun Inventory Strategy for Solo Mode

When you enter the map, you are given a pickaxe and a backpack to hold your inventory. There are 5 spaces to fill with things like gear and weapons, and another location in your pack for storing ammo and building materials. While you can only hold on to 5 weapons of shields, you can hold almost one thousand rounds of ammo for a given weapon and for building materials. Your pickaxe is assigned the primary spot on your inventory, and it is wise to keep it there. It is not an effective weapon, but it is important to have easy access to help you gather materials when you encounter them.

You will have default keys or buttons that will help you quickly access the weapons you assign to the different slots. Know these keys by heart and always line up your inventory the same way each time so it does not require you to think when you need to make fast decisions. For example, keep the pickaxe in slot #1, and then always put an AR in #2, and a sniper in #3. Add another weapon to slot #3, preferably a close- or mid-range option, and reserve the last 2 spots for meds and shields.

- Short-range guns include pistols, revolvers, shotguns, AR burst, and SMG's.

- Mid-range guns include: pistols, revolvers, AR scope, and SMG's

- Long-range guns include: sniper, AR, grenade launcher

For long range, the sniper is the best option. If you have not practiced with a sniper rifle yet, consider trying to stick to semi-automatic. This way you have more rounds in the magazine. This will give you more practice. If you are skilled with sniping, pick up the bolt-action so you can inflict the most damage per shot.

If you are not able to get a sniper, a hunting rifle is another good option. It is considered to be in the middle between the sniper and an AR. Their accuracy is better and the bullet drop is not as extreme, making it good for both mid- and long-range. Crossbows are another type of sniper, but they are not as dangerous or advantageous. If you are strapped for a long-range weapon, you can pick this up; otherwise, choose another sniper option over the crossbow.

AR's are the weapon of choice for many. They are deadly and somewhat accurate. They are also more common on the map. Chances are good that these will be the first weapon to get and use. AR's and Bursts are excellent but require more skill in aiming. A missed burst could be fatal to you. And SMG and a Tactical SMG inflict some good damage but are only helpful in close range. Because of this limited functionality, you should choose other versions of an AR over an SMG or Tactical SMG. SCAR would be the best AR you can get your hands on. They inflict the most damage and are the most accurate.

Shotguns are powerful weapons for in-your-face battle. In solo play, having two shotguns side by side in your inventory is helpful because you can do the infamous "double pump." This means you can fire your first shotgun and switch to your second as the first reload. This way there is no lag time between reloads and you can inflict the most damage on your opponent. It is not as effective as it used to be since some of the latest updates, but it can still be a beneficial strategy in your inventory. For example, if you have a tactical and a pump shotgun in your inventory, consider placing them side-by-side. When engaging an opponent, fire the first shot with the pump, trying to hit the head. After the first shot, move to your tactical shotgun. This way, if the shot misses the head and only lowers their overall health, you can move in with the tactical. If you land the headshot with the pump, you will have immediately defeated your enemy.

Explosives are great to have in your inventory, but keep those for later in the mid- and late-game. You want them to take down buildings or annihilate your rival. When you are facing more skilled and stocked opponents, these are handy to do a lot of damage quickly.

Meds and shields should be in your inventory, too. As any pro player will tell you, you need to be able to restore your health and protect yourself, and these are the best ways to do it. Use a med pack or bandage to bring up your health or drink a shield potion to allow you to take fire without losing valuable health. There is a variance in an opinion which is better to keep in your inventory at all times, or what to drop if you come across more meds. Some pros like to have med kits over minis, while others like chug jugs. You will find what you use and like the most as you keep practicing.

Also, having building materials on hand to throw up a wall or ramp is critical to gaining the high ground and winning. This means your inventory needs to have as much as possible of every type of material. Wood gains full health the fastest, making it a powerful tool in a gunfight, but metal will hold up to the most blasts, even though it takes the longest to reach full health.

Gunplay for Solo Mode

Playing by yourself means you get to win by yourself. It is only your skills and tactics that got you to the final spot. But getting there is no easy feat, and even people that have logged hours of game time still cannot reach this sacred ground. How do you get there? Simple, follow these tips below to help you get there every time:

1. Land quickly

The faster you can get to the ground, the faster you can get a weapon. This means you want to jump earlier in the battle bus's flight. But when you jump, make sure it is over a flat, low-lying ground, such as a river or plains. Do not jump out over a hill or mountain or even tall buildings and trees. This is because your glider will auto-deploy at a certain height. It will deploy earlier over higher ground. If you are jumping by the edge of the map, head towards the ocean so you can get as low as possible. And once you land, do not feel the need to loot the entire building. Grab what you need and move on.

2. Attack with Aggression

Your best option is to be offensive. When you see someone, attack before they see you. It only takes one good headshot to kill a rival, so do not hesitate. If you take them off-guard, they are more likely to make a mistake.

This is also a good way to practice your weapon skills.

3. Get Up High

143

Getting up high means 2 things; you can see them better and you can increase the odds of landing a headshot. When you find someone that is at your same height or up higher, either find a spot higher than them or build it. Also, when you enter a building, start from the top or roof and work your way down, rather than entering from the bottom.

4. Predict the Path

This means predicting 2 things: the path of the storm and the path of the other players. This means that you need to know where you are at on the map and where you think the center of the circle will be in. Think about the major named areas on the map that you can go through on the way to the center of the circle. Also, keep in mind that other players will be doing the same, moving in with you. This allows you to engage in fights or avoid them.

5. Have Plenty of Supplies

Being able to shoot is important, but many pros will argue that being able to build is more important. You definitely have more control over a build than a shot. In combat, you can create significant advantage and protection. Make sure to have at least one hundred of each material when entering the late-game. This is because each wall takes 10 materials, so having this can help by preventing a shortage while building in a fight. So as you move through the map, harvest trees and cars as go. Do not waste time, but grab a good amount as you seek your next kill.

Make sure that you keep your health high and stock up on shields. This way, if you get into a fight that is a surprise or extra aggressive, you can heal yourself before moving on.

Early-game

Now that you have landed, you must grab a gear. If you are not practicing fighting skills, try to land in a remote area. This way you can focus on gearing up and taking out unsuspecting rivals. Harvest materials on the way to the closest house, and pick up gears from the buildings. If you have to land in an area with a lot of people, grab the first gun you can get your hands on and fight. When they clear out or die, grab the rest of the loot available and get moving. The game is about to enter the mid-game status.

Mid-game

The circle begins closing in, sending the game into the mid-gameplay. Watch the circle and predict where the center will be. At this point in the game, you do not need to be in the circle, but you should be headed that way. If you happened to land in the circle, bunker in and do not engage others until you have to. Find a hiding place, like a large bush, and stay hidden. Hiding does not mean you can engage an enemy easily, do not shoot unless being shot at.

Late-game

If you are hiding and the circle starts closing in, move fast to another spot. Watch where the majority of the other players will be coming in from and try to stay away from them. If you are in the center, use this knowledge to start taking them out as they enter the center. If you find yourself entering along with the others, try to be one of the last to get inside. This way they take the brunt of the fire before you get there. If you are entering from a quieter part of the map, try to keep out of sight and stay away from the crowd. If you can get in under the radar, you can find a good spot to hide or snipe your rivals. When the game starts to boil down to just a few of you, you will need to become more and more aggressive, moving faster into the circle and start building. You will encounter people who have hid the entire game and are now building up. These people are nicknamed "builders" for a reason. Their sole aim the whole game was to get to this point and out-build you to get the advantage. If you have a rocket launcher or grenade launcher, this is the time to use it. If not, consider hiding and waiting them out. Let the others attack the builders and stay out of sight.

The final 5 players mean you are in the winning lot. Hiding is still a good strategy here, as the others will be looking for one another, too. If at all possible, let those other four battle until you can come in and take out the last one standing while they are low on health. Then you have your victory royale. If you cannot stay hidden, make sure you have cover nearby as you attack. If you have to choose, target the player that has the best advantage, such as the person that is the highest. Ideally, you want the last 2 players besides yourself to fight it out, and then swoop in for the final kill. If you find yourself in the match, it will come down to skill and luck. Much of this situation is based on luck of the circle, but the person that can play without panicking will most likely be the victor. So do not panic and enjoy the win as your reward.

Chapter 7
Squad Mode

Choosing to play with trusted and skilled friends is a great way to have fun and get some wins under your belt. This is not only because you have allies on the field, but also because you have combined resources, too. But keep in mind, so does everyone else. Playing squad mode is very different than playing solo. If you want to win like a pro every time, it is important for you and your squad play it smart.

Gun Inventory Strategy for Squad Mode

Like playing in solo mode, you need to stock your inventory well, but now it is not just you loading up on weapons. Maybe you can handle face-to-face combat well, and know your way around a shotgun, but your friend is a talented sniper. This means you no longer need to save a space in your inventory for a long-range weapon. Instead, consider having designated roles for each of you. Have a few shotguns in your arsenal and leave the sniping to your teammate. Also, the same goes for building materials. If you do not enjoy or are not good at building, consider having a builder designated on your squad. This does not mean you should forgo having your own supply of materials, but it does mean you should not be the one holding the majority of them. Assigning roles like this can help you determine how your inventories will be set up.

Close-Range Squad Member

You have 5 slots to fill; fill at least 4 of them with close-range weapons like a tactical SMG or shotguns. Of course, every inventory should have at least 1 AR, because it is so versatile, even at close-range if needed. But occasionally you may need to engage at medium-range and this may save your life. If possible, SCAR is the ideal weapon to put in your inventory. The final slot you must fill with meds or shields. Ammo is just as critical as before, so make sure you are always gathering as much as you can. A face-to-face battle is something you need to approach as a distraction while your squad members flank your enemy and take them out by surprise, but this strategy will put you in harm's way. You will need the ammo to battle well but the meds or shields will keep you protected.

Medium-Range Squad Member

A squad member fighting at medium-range should be someone who can fight close or far away. They can run up behind an enemy while your close-range squad member is attacking to flank them and try to take out the rest of the enemy squad as well as the 1 engaged in the fight. To have a good inventory, a medium-range squad member should always have an AR in the first inventory slot and a few other medium-to long-range weapons on hand. Stock a building-buster, like a rocket launcher or minigun, to help break down barriers or send an enemy squad running. Another amazing weapon to put in inventory as a medium-range weapon is a silenced gun, like a suppressed SMG or handgun. This gives you the advantage of hiding while the others are engaged. You can choose between taking them out loud and fast, or sneaking up on them and taking them out one at a time before the rest of the squad of other rivals realizes what is going on.

Long-Range Squad Member

Snipers are a must have for a squad member who is designated for long-range firing. Most likely you will post up in a high position and survey the area. Your job will be to take out rivals as they approach or before they can spot your squads' position. Sometimes you will be separated from your squad, such as when they are in a building or they are constructing a tower. You will choose another high ground opposite the structure, with a good overall vantage point, and take out anyone approaching. Fill up the majority of your slots with long-range weapons and a few medium- to long-range weapons, like a rocket or grenade launcher or an AR. As your squad enters the end-game, you may not rely as heavily on long-range snipers as you will with your medium- to long-range options, such as the AR. If possible, try to get a SCAR AR for yourself, as well as for your close-range teammate.

As with any inventory, no matter the type of game, you need to make sure you all have a sufficient supply of ammo and building materials. A long-range squad member may not need as many building supplies as a close-range but they will still be necessary for the mid- and late-game. Do not pass up an ammo box or miss the chance to gather wood, brick, or stone.

Swapping materials and weapons

Another advantage squad mode provides is the ability to share supplies and weapons with one another. To share resources, open up your inventory and select the item you wish to share. This could be anything from a weapon to ammo or building materials. Once you select the items to drop for your squad mates, hit "X' and let it go. This can vary depending on if you are playing on a console, PC or mobile, but in general, it is the same process. Practice with your squad to share resources with one another early in the game so when you reach the end-game, you can quickly pass what the other needs and vice versa.

Communication is essential in between your squad members, especially when it comes to finding materials and weapons. This means if you are apart from one another looting, you each should be talking about what you are finding. Ask if your squad members need an SMG or grenade launcher. Find out if they are well-stocked on wood or ammo. The more open the communication, the better prepared you all will be for the fighting and the end-game.

Gunplay for Squad Mode

In general, you will want to stick with your squadmates, but that being said, you also do not want to be shoulder-to-shoulder running through the field together. This makes you one big, easy target. Instead, keep some distance between the 3 of you, and stagger your progression, keeping one ahead and one behind. In this way, if the front man, typically your close-range member, starts taking fire, the other two can swing wide around, find the opponent and take them out instead of being easy target practice as a clump.

A benefit of playing squad mode is that you can revive one another. This is a great tool to help keep your whole team alive as long as possible, but do not risk your own safety trying to help another teammate. Wait until it is safe for you to approach and revive so you do not open yourself up to an attack. This is why each squad member should always have meds or shields in their inventory.

Keep in mind that all your fighting strategies are options for your enemies as well. You are not always going to be fighting against a full squad, because some squads will lose their members, but it is almost impossible for you to know if the 1 person engaging in the fight is alone or they have 2 other squad members trying to flank you as well. The best way to know is their behavior. A squad that is down 1 or 2 players will be more defensive and passive typically than a group that has all their members. Also, if you take down a rival and they immediately disappear you can be sure that they no longer have any other squad members left on the map. They were the last 1 and you just took them out, therefore you do not need to look for others hiding in the bushes or running up to flank you.

Sometimes you will need to build to get the advantage in a fight. This is best left to your most skilled builder on the squad; someone who can throw up a good and strong structure fast. Do not try to build it together, as it will most likely cause confusion and result in you not getting a solid tower or opening you and your squad member up to fire. Depending on where the enemy is located, you will then want to place the appropriate squad member in the tower while the other two try to get around the enemy and take them out from the wings. For example, if there is an enemy squad advancing on you at close-range, have your close-range member in the tower, raining down fire on the other group. This will give the rest of your squad time to run in opposite directions, diverting other enemies from the fight or eluding them so you can get the advantage. If the rival squad is mid-range or long-range, place your long-range member in the tower and have the other 2 work out the strategy for the attack. Occasionally, you will need all hands in the fight, but for the most part, you can divide and conquer.

Early-game

The way you start the game is how you set the tone for the rest of the match. This means, in the lobby, your squad should be talking about how you want to play the game, who will take on what role, where to land, and any other pertinent information.

Make sure each squad member is aware of the plan before boarding the battle bus. When your squad members jump, you need to jump with them so you all land in the same place. If you have decided to be more aggressive, this may mean you are headed to a heavy-loot spot. If you are being more passive, you are going to a less-populated location. Once you land on the ground, you need to move to get the supplies and weapons. Communicate constantly with one another about what you are finding and things you are choosing to leave behind. This way no one is lacking. If you are coming up to a named location on the map, known for its loot, it could be a good strategy to get up in a tree or build a quick snipers nest so that you can take out enemies as they leave a building loaded with loot. If you send someone into the building to clear it, let the other 2 keep enemies out. Once the building is clear, you can take turns running in to grab items your squad will need before moving on to the next location. This strategy will help keep you all protected as much as possible.

Mid-game

Keep your back to the water and choose to run along the edge of the storm or sprint to the center. This will depend if your squad is playing aggressive or not and how close you are to the center already. If you find yourself far from the center, consider playing the edge for the first storm. If you are close to the center, start building up to take advantage of the situation. While you are building a structure to fortify your squad, place your sniper in a location across from your tower so they can defend you as you build and can take out advancing enemies by surprise. The mid-game tends to slow down, so use this time to share resources and gather what you need to make it through to the end. It is very important that you all have enough supplies to make it through the late-game, so now is the time to harvest. It is a good strategy to wait for looters after a kill to take them out unsuspecting and take all the loot you need.

Late-game

When you are facing only a handful of players and the storm closes in faster and faster with more damage, hiding along the edges is not always the best strategy. Instead, the late-game is time to use speed and aggression to win. This means you can engage bases if you have plenty of building busters like a minigun, rocket launcher or grenades or you can build your own tower and defend it against the other players. Some pros suggest playing it safe until the top 10, while others like to start this aggressive play at 20 or 25. It is up to you and your squad, as well as determined by the number of resources you have. No matter your position, aim to be in the last 3, allowing the other 2 squads to battle it out. Keep your squad out of sight of the other two, while setting up position up high to advance in for the final kill. If you find yourself in the middle of the fight but 1 squad still out there, splitting your members up to search for the other group is a good idea. You never want to lose sight of the remaining opponents. If possible, try to push them towards the final fight, so you can get the other two fighting one another while you slink back to wait it out. Once the winner of that fight finished you need to be ready to immediately engage. Do not allow them time to fortify or heal. Take all the advantage you can get, play aggressively and go for the final kill for your squad's Victory Royale.

Conclusion

Thanks for making it through to the end of *Fortnite: Battle Royale: The Ultimate Guide to Improve Your Gunplay for Winning EVERY BATTLE ROYALE Like a Pro,* let's hope it was informative and able to provide you with all of the tools you need to achieve your goals whatever they may be.

The next step is to log in to your account and start customizing your settings to support your aggressive fighting goal. Tweak you in and out of game settings to help you aim and move with precision. Then, get in the game and start practicing. Practice firing different guns, fighting styles, and cover. Play it safe and play it aggressively. Be stealthy and then in-your-face. The more you practice the better you will get, but make sure you are practicing with a purpose. Practice for the win so you can stand victorious each and every time you log in.

Hopefully, you have learned some interesting tips and techniques you can employ in your gaming to push yourself to the next level. Make sure you get in the game and try out different suggestions to find what works for you, your squad, and your goals. When you are comfortable with your controls and know how to approach a rival you will win every fight and find yourself boosting your stats like a pro. Now, put down this book, log into Fortnite: Battle Royale and start shooting!

Finally, if you found this book useful in any way, a review on Amazon is always appreciated!

Book - III

Fortnite: Battle Royale

Advanced Tips, Tricks, and Map Strategies from Elite Players to WIN #1 VICTORY ROYALE!

By

Pro Gamer Guide

Introduction

Congratulations and thank you for downloading *Fortnite Battle Royale: Advanced Tips, Tricks, and Map Strategies from Elite Players to WIN #1 VICTORY ROYALE!* The world of gaming is growing increasingly chaotic and downloading this book is the first step you can take towards actually doing something about it. The first step is also always the easiest, however, which is why the information you find in the following chapters is so important to take to heart as they are not concepts that can be put into action immediately. If you file them away for when they are really needed, however, then when the time comes to actually use them, you will be glad you did.

To that end, the following chapters will discuss the primary preparedness principals that you will need to consider if you ever hope to really be ready for scoring a win in the most popular game of the last year. This means you will want to consider the quality of your building including the potential issues raised by its current location, how it can be best utilized in an emergency, and various reinforcements or fortifications you may need to have on hand in case of an emergency.

With shelter out of the way, you will then learn everything you need to know about fighting other players. Rounding out the three primary requirements for successful survival, you will then learn about crucial materials storage principles and what they will mean for you. Finally, you will learn the 10 secrets every Fortnite players must know in order to be successful during the battle.

There are plenty of books on this subject on the market, so thanks again for choosing this one! Every effort was made to ensure it is full of as much useful information as possible. Please enjoy!

Chapter 1
How it all began

Battle Royale and Fortnite: How a Phenomenon of Hundreds of Millions was Born

From a film with Kitano, we have moved on to a global phenomenon born almost by chance that today involves millions of people. From the boy to the international stars, the story of Battle Royale is the story of those phenomena of success that you cannot predict until you find yourself being the only one who does not understand what you are talking about while everyone around you is talking about it and suddenly you feel old. Because you do not know what Fortnite is, you have no idea what PUBG means and why Griezmann dances like a fool when he scores.

With Battle Royale, we mean a very precise type of game whose name should already have made everyone understand the gamers who also have a passion for Japanese cinema. The name comes from a Japanese film of 2000, inspired by a book with the same title, with the participation of Takeshi Kitano. In the film, a whole class of particularly riotous Japanese students is abandoned on a desert island. Each of them has some ration, a map, a compass and a weapon randomly assigned. The last one that survives wins, all the others must die.

In the intentions of the author, Battle Royale wanted to be a fierce and satirical critique of the adult world—to dispose of the future of young people without caring too much about the consequences. Curiously today, the same name is associated with something that is misunderstood by adults and loved by boys, and that is making some of them make a lot of money.

The concept of this mode is not new in the gaming industry: the online shooters have always offered modes called "The last man standing," but until now it was almost always clashes between a few players in fairly small maps.

Then came Hunger Games which brought to the general public the idea of a group of boys ready to kill themselves in a violent way for the public, and this led to the development of a modification for Minecraft entitled as the film, in which more players had to eliminate until the last survivor crowned the winner. The mode quickly became popular on YouTube and this led to emulation in other games, one of which was Arma 2, an extremely accurate war simulator with huge maps. In this case, the mod was called "Battle Royale" and was developed by Brendan Greene, whose online pseudonym was "PlayerUnknown."

His idea is not to put much of the resources at the center of the map like in Hunger Games but instead spread them around the game environment.

One day, Brendan became the creative director in a small software house called Bluehole and started working on PUBG—or PlayerUnknown's BattleGrounds—the game responsible for blowing up the genre and making it a show for millions of players and spectators. The graphics are cheap; they are malevolent and have no history—only a hundred people who from time to time try to kill each other in a map that shrinks more and more. To see it from outside it seems like nothing but instead will become the engine of a new millionaire phenomenon.

Curiously, in this case, there is much similarity with League of Legends—one of the most important titles in the export scene: both are born from a "mod" of a previous game, both were almost completely ignored until their player base suddenly exploded, and both were copied.

In the case of PUBG, we are talking about Fortnite, announced a few years ago quietly as an online cooperative title of Epic Games, a name that carries no great weight until the Battle Royale variant came out. The game is visually more beautiful, optimized, and colorful than PUBG. You can buy aesthetic changes to make your character more picturesque and, compared to PUBG, also allows you to build structures and—above all—it's free.

The Fortnite Phenomenon

From that moment began a long run that has culminated in overtaking the last few months that has made Fortnite a phenomenon much more global than you can think, especially since both games can also be played on mobile devices.

At the moment, Fortnite peaks at 3.4 million players at any one time. It has become a money machine thanks to people who buy game items (reaching revenues of $223 million only in March) and also due to some unsuspecting fans: footballers, NBA stars who want customized shoes on the theme of the game, or singers like Drake.

When the singer played a game in streaming with the most famous player of Fortnite, Ninja, a guy who earns crazy figures with this title, they were watched by more than 600,000 people. And here we return to the footballer Griezmann who does a strange dance called "Take the L" which was later taken by one of the animations of the game.

The game's impact on the global market is so large that even a superpower like Marvel had to deal with it and launched a collaboration at the launch of *Avengers: Infinity War* to include Thanos, the big bad of the Marvel Cinematic Universe, into the game. The game's media dominance even led Activision to launch a Battle Royale mode in the next Call of Duty, which had to bow to the new idols of the youth.

Its climax: Epic Games decided to invest $100 million in prize money to be used for tournaments. The total prize money of the previous year's top titles barely even reach the same figure. When we talk about Fortnite, everything touches the absurd so much that for many, this bubble will not last forever. Maybe it will be so, but for now, it is surely the favorite game of millions who play to have fun, laugh, share, talk and spend. It is easy to prove it—winning is difficult—but survival dynamics always make it exciting until the next phenomenon that nobody has foreseen will come.

The Game

Fortnite is undoubtedly the hit game par excellence, at least according to data available for the first few months of 2018. The Battle Royale mode was developed and then released independently by Epic Games, managing to attract the attention of the players but also of the analysts of the sector, of sports apparently very far from video games, and even of artists and singers. In this book, you can find everything you need to know about Fortnite: from general information to specifications, weekly challenges, to instructions for use.

Fortnite: Battle Royale is an online third-person shooter: the aim is to shoot everything that moves in order to be the last alive in the map. However, part of the success of the game is also due to a fairly innovative proposal in the gameplay: combining the action of gunplay with a building mechanic, thanks to a menu that very closely resembles the one of Minecraft. Here, you collect useful weapons and tools, shoot, hide and use the environment to your advantage; at the same time, it is possible to play as a team of four, exploring the map and building structures to help each other along the way.

Fortnite was developed through the collaboration between Epic Games and People Can Fly. The former then thought about its publication—first as a title in early access on all platforms, then free-to-play in 2018. Fortnite can be played without spending a penny, with the exception of microtransactions which are only focused on cosmetics. The PvE mode, called Save the World, is currently priced at 39.99 Euro but will soon become free-to-play for all players.

The Game Modes

Fortnite presents two distinct game modes: Battle Royale and Save the World. It was the former which became the reason behind its success around the globe because it was fast-paced, adrenaline-inducing, sufficiently strategic, and above all free-to-play.

Battle Royale begins with 100 players aboard the Battlebus, a bus strapped onto a balloon. The players are then thrown into battle on the island below. The map turns into a battlefield as soon as the players land. All the players will be constantly fighting each other. One player will remain standing to win the

Victory Royale. During the battle, each player can use a pickaxe to gather resources, erect buildings, or get new weapons by finding better equipment around. These are all essential game elements for survival.

Save the World is based not on competition but rather on cooperation: teams of four players must work together to stop waves of aliens who, in a post-apocalyptic future, have conquered our planet. To achieve this, it is necessary to use building to erect defensive structures, place traps, and fire against the invaders. Completing the proposed missions increases the player's skills and unlocks interesting bonuses.

The game map of Battle Royale mixes openly flat environments with more mountainous areas. There is also a river that flows from north to south, complete with a lake in the middle. There are also some points of interest such as cities, rural areas, laboratories, hangars, and forests. Wherever it is possible to find new weapons or basic tools for survival, the user is urged to move continuously to grab as much loot as possible, which will naturally also represent the main objective of his opponents: the battle is inevitable.

Fortnite presents weapons divided by levels of rarity: uncommon, common, rare, epic and legendary. The difference naturally concerns the damage inflicted by each of them, in addition to the rate of fire, the range, and accuracy. But the crates and loot on the map can also hide equally important consumables: for example, bandages, med kits, and potions of various kinds, which allow you to heal yourself, recover hit points and get bonuses for your protection. Finally, a third useful tool in Battle Royale are the traps, which can be accumulated indefinitely without taking up space in the inventory. There are good not only to damage opponents but also to build useful platforms, for example, to get to higher areas or escape the storm.

How to Download Fortnite

All your friends do nothing but talk about Fortnite, a video game available for computers, PlayStation 4 and Xbox One. To make it particularly interesting are the cartoony art style and the completely different game setting in every game—but above all is its cost: free. What do you say? You cannot wait to get involved but would you like some tips on how to download Fortnite? Lucky for you, you've come to the right guide!

Get comfortable and do not waste any more time in chatter. Take five minutes of free time, read the next paragraphs carefully and you will find how to download and install Fortnite on your computer or on your console: I assure you that in less than no time you can start

playing with your friends. Good reading, and above all, have fun!

How to Download Fortnite on Your Computer

Unlike many video games, Fortnite is not available on digital distribution platforms like Steam, but you can download it for free from the official website of its manufacturer.

Before going into detail about the procedure for downloading and installing Fornite, you need to know the minimum requirements necessary for the operation of the game and compare them with the specifications of your computer.

- Operating system: Windows 7 64-bit, macOS Sierra
- Processor: Core i5 2.4 GHz
- Memory: 4 GB
- Video card: Intel HD 4000
- Free disk space: 15 GB

For a better gaming experience, you must have a computer with the following recommended requirements:

- Operating system: Windows 7 64-bit, macOS Sierra

- Processor: Core i5 2.8 GHz
- Memory: 16 GB
- Video card: Nvidia GT 650, AMD Radeon HD 7870
- Free disk space: 20 GB

After making sure that your computer has the minimum requirements to play Fortnite, you can proceed with the download and installation of the Epic Games Launcher, the software necessary to download Fortnite and play with it.

Connect to the Epic Games website and click on the Download button on the main screen. Alternatively, click on *Get Fortnite* placed in the top menu and click on the Download button. Now, click on the Login button, enter your details in the Username and Password fields and click on the Login button to access your account.

If you do not have an account yet, press the Login buttons on Facebook and Google to link to Epic Games your social account, otherwise fill out the form to register via email. Then enter your details in the fields Name, Surname, Display name (minimum 3 and maximum 16 characters), Email and Password, then check the next to the item I read and accept the terms of service and click on the button Create account.

Within a few moments, you will receive an email containing a link to verify your identity: press the Check email button to complete the activation procedure.

After creating your account, it will automatically start the game download. If not, on the new open page, press the Windows or Mac buttons to manually start the download of the Epic Games launcher.

Once the download is complete, you can proceed with the installation of the game on your computer. If you have a Windows PC, double-click on the *EpicInstaller-[version]-fortnite.msi* file and press the Run and Install buttons then wait for the installation and download of the updates to complete and the game will be done.

If you're using a Mac, open the .dmg package you just downloaded and drag the Epic Games Launcher icon to the MacOS Applications folder. Open the Applications folder, right-click on the Epic Games Launcher icon, and click on the Open item to launch it.

Download Fortnite

After installing and downloading the files necessary for the launcher to work, you can finally start downloading Fortnite. In the new window, enter your login information, check the check mark next to the item Remember Me (so you do not have to log in every time) and then log in.

Make sure you are on the Fortnite screen, press the green Install button, check the required tick to accept the license agreement and click the Accept button. Choose the folder and the installation path. If you want, you can check Automatic updates. Click Install to start downloading Fortnite.

As mentioned above, the game occupies a disk space of about 15 GB and therefore the download may take a few hours of time especially if your connection is not fast. While waiting, you can view the progress of the download, the data downloaded, press the Pause button to temporarily stop the download, or press the X button to cancel the operation.

When the download is complete, press the Start button to start playing. If you want to uninstall the game, you can click on the gear wheel icon and select Remove.

Fortnite is also available for free for the latest generation of consoles such as PlayStation 4 and Xbox One, and the download and installation process is almost identical for both gaming systems.

If you have a PS4, select the toolbox icon to access Settings, press on Network and Configure Internet connection and choose the type of connection between Use Wi-Fi and Use a network cable (LAN).

After connecting the console to the Internet, go to the menu Settings > Account Management > Access PlayStation Network and connect to your account by entering your login details in the login ID and password fields, while if you do not have an account, press on new user entry. Create an account and click on the Subscribe Now option to create one.

Now, press the icon of the shopping bag to access the PlayStation Store, press the Search item and type Fortnite in the search field, then press the Download button to start the download. To learn more, read my guide on how to play online on PS4.

If you're using an Xbox One to play, make sure your console is connected to the Internet, otherwise press the Xbox button on the controller and go to Settings > All Settings > Network > Network Settings and select the Configure Wireless Network item. Now, click on the Log in button on the home screen and enter your login details to connect to your account: if you do not have one yet, you can read my in-depth guide.

To start downloading Fortnite, launch the Xbox Store, press the search button, search Fortnite and press the button to download the game. When the download is complete, the video game will be available in the list of games available on your Xbox One.

Fortnite vs PUBG: Which is better and why?

Is there room for both on the battlefield? Let's try comparing.

Unless you live on Mars, in a cave, or without Wi-Fi, you will have heard about the resounding success of PlayerUnknown's Battlegrounds.

At the height of its popularity, in December 2017, 30 million players were ready to challenge each other for the first place—a crazy number. Shortly before the official release of the game, however, another title began to make its way among the players: Fortnite: Battle Royale. PUBG purists kept their distance, but despite everything else in the world, they immediately jumped on what became the game of the moment. Before starting our comparison, it is worth pointing out that this is just the beginning: even the biggest publishers want a slice of the battle royale cake.

Differences

We talk about the differences between the two despite the basic elements in common, starting from simple numbers: in both Fortnite and PUBG, you have 60 seconds of "warm-up" pre-game. Then there are 100 players who are "dumped" onto an island. Finally, the battle starts all against all, with each user on equal terms: arsenal and equipment are present on the battlefield and must be sought during the game. In both of them, in the long run, you get tired of always sifting through the same areas, but fortunately, we get strange atmospheric phenomena or new maps to refresh the experience. Another common denominator is the victory awarded to the last survivor, be it the "Winner winner chicken dinner" of PUBG or the "Victory Royale" of Fortnite.

Graphics

In the chest of both pulsates a heart based on Unreal Engine 4, but also here there is no shortage of differences. Fortnite has a cartoon look, winking at Team Fortress 2, and its construction mechanics recall another world success, Minecraft. PUBG has a more serious aspect, deriving from the Arma 2 war simulator and the DayZ mod. A seriousness is also maintained in the graphics and atmosphere, although there will always be some idiot ready to break that austerity typical of military-style games, perhaps holding the now iconic pan. The first aims at total lightness, the second wants to leave a good impression visually, as can also be seen from the speakers in which both hide the loot: the boxes of Fortnite seem to come out of a Legend of Zelda randomly, while in PUBG you have to scour houses abandoned and disused warehouses. From this, Fortnite indicates more precisely the effectiveness of a weapon, suggesting immediately that the one that is gripped is weaker or stronger, thus saving space on the inventory, and therefore also time, which is not underestimated.

Ballistics

Two worlds apart, as if they were Schwarzenegger and DeVito in "The Twins": PUBG points to hard and pure realism, while Fortnite to the pure arcade experience, with only a few weapons with bullets that follow a more realistic ballistic, while most pump guns use hitscan. Bloom also exists, a precision mechanic linked to a percentage of possibilities. In PUBG, it is difficult to understand if the projectile will arrive at its destination, and in every kill, the player's ability to identify the behavior of a weapon/projectile also comes into play. Locating and following a target, firing quick but precise shots, and managing the trajectory of projectiles are all fundamental skills, especially for high-level games. Also crucial to master are the various modes of fire and alternating them at the right time, particularly when approaching one of the many vehicles whose maps are swarming.

Tactics

If PUBG is full of vehicles, Fortnite compensates with verticality. The pure use of guns, grenades, and traps do not win the games. Instead, knowing how to build intelligently will greatly influence the outcome of a match. Try not to die falling from a structure too high, which unfortunately happens very often, and not to distract while collecting the resources necessary for construction. It may cost you your life. PUBG, on the other hand, cannot go beyond the usual "dances," typical of every shooter, things already done hundreds of times: we hide, we study the various areas that we want to loot before going into action, we come out of the corners very carefully.

Is the price (and support) right?

Obviously, with the fact that behind PUBG is an independent team, while behind Fortnite a triple-A company, the technical quality and frequency of updates are certainly unequal. PUBG is known for its PC optimization problems, not to mention the mobile and Xbox One versions. It has improved a lot in recent times, but it is still far from perfect. Glitches, hackers, and crashes continue to undermine the gaming experience.

Even Fortnite suffers from framerate drops and technical problems, but it is undoubtedly more refined. At the same time, however, despite the economic and numerical differences, PUBG has allowed the development team to grow disproportionately and to be able to intervene with a very high frequency on the game between fixes and optimizations now per week, while Fortnite, published as a game at all the effects, requires many more certifications and "bureaucracy" before being able to receive an update. But when you look at the price, it is clear who ticks: playing Fortnite will not really cost you anything, and even on PC you will not have many problems to run it. And on consoles, it will be great. PUBG has a non-indifferent entry cost, lower than usual but still present. And to enjoy it, fully you need a good PC or an Xbox One X since on the Xbox One, the problems are still very serious.

Conclusion

Despite competing in the same sub-genre, the differences that make PUBG and Fortnite unique still exist. The most hardcore players, attentive to realism and the most difficult and complex gameplay, will do well to point their eyes on PUBG, perhaps waiting for the team to fix the problems mentioned. At the same time, however, Fortnite can be appreciated and can be a sort of additive appetizer just to PUBG. Its winning element, in addition to price, is the building component, which makes it truly unique in the modern shooter scene, and is part, perhaps, of its incredible success. In short, we can consider it a draw: it will be only your taste that decrees the real winner. Clearly, since this is a Fortnite book, the focus will be on this game.

Chapter 2
General Advice

Building on the success of the genre after the phenomenon of PlayerUnknown's Battlegrounds, Fortnite arrived on the PC and console market, immediately gathering the approval of millions of players who decided to try the Epic Games title.

Through this guide, we're going to provide you with some guidelines and some tips to help you get the most out of Fortnite: Battle Royale.

General Advice

- Avoid advancing in the open field: using any type of cover to move around the map is essential to avoid becoming an easy prey for opponents. Take advantage, therefore, of trees, buildings, rock walls and anything else you find nearby.
- Once you reach the safety zone bounded by the circle on the mini-map, do not make the mistake of lowering your guard: the enemies may come from any direction, since some of them may still be outside the area of salvation. Try to ambush those who should arrive after you, perhaps even exploiting, in this case, the cover that the map offers you.
- When you feel the presence of a shootout, you could instinctively and unwisely immerse yourself immediately

in the battle. Our advice is to evaluate the situation, as far as possible, before moving on to action. Act at the end of the battle and eliminate the already-injured enemies. This could turn out to be a very smart move, which could also guarantee you loot interesting things.

- If you need resources, visit buildings and facilities scattered around the map. You will have to act, as usual, with complete caution, since even the other players, if necessary, will venture into these places.

- Do not underestimate the strategic role that can cover the doors of buildings. Once inside, close the door to mislead the opponents to suggest that the structure you are in is still abandoned. If the trap will work, it will be easy at this point to attack those who have naively approached.

- As with any shooter, we recommend diversifying your arsenal. Have shotguns, sniper rifles, and so on. It goes without saying that the med-kits can be literally life-saving and that it is always good to collect them together with minor cure power.

- We also suggest that you use the headphones during your games. In Fortnite, players' footsteps are much more distinct than most other titles, an aspect that, when exploited in the right way, could prove to be of crucial importance.

- Track or escape from enemies. To track down your enemies, Fortnite provides a series of clues from which to take inspiration. As we have already said, it is good to listen carefully to the steps of the other players, but also pay attention to the dusty trail that these cause on the ground as they pass. In addition to this, examine the projectiles you would find on the ground, potentially revealing the opponent's nearest position. In case you are in a moment of escape, it may be useful to climb on one of the surrounding buildings. To help you in this sense, you could find piles of tires, which can be useful to give you the momentum to cling to the protrusions of the structures.

- A good way to hide your presence is to crouch.

- By pressing the top arrow of the D-Pad of your controller, you will be able to open and consult the game map. Use it constantly to better plan your actions.

- Fortnite does not use vehicles, but at the same time has much narrower maps compared to PUBG. From this, it is easier to avoid the fatal "storm," whose range of action is indicated in the mini-map. If you find yourself within the perturbation, do not panic: just as happens in the Bluehole title, even in Fortnite your character will be able to resist for a certain period of time while his health is slowly reduced, leaving you in this way the time to react.

- Regarding the storm, staying on the edge of it could guarantee you a tactical advantage, succeeding from here to attack the players involved in crossing the line to the safe zone.

- If you are accustomed to the clashes of PUBG, you will have to change your approach in Fortnite. As mentioned, the maps will be more restricted, and the clashes much more frequent.

- Sift through each building visited to find the treasure chests: it is within them that you will find the rarest weapons and the most precious objects, so do not be afraid to break down the interior walls that, perhaps, could hide rarities.

- If it is not too risky, always remember to examine the bodies of the downed opponents; you could find weapons, ammunition, and other items. Like, for example, in MMOs, Fortnite also has three levels of weapon and equipment rarity. In ascending order, we find grey, blue, green, purple and orange. The rarer a weapon is, the higher the DPS (damage per second) will be, along with other improved statistics.

- By taking advantage of the game's building mechanic, you will be able to put on bridges, small shacks, and towers to have a strategic advantage over your opponents. Since the circle of the storm is constantly moving, it would be a waste of resources to install the buildings in the early stages of the match; act on the contrary in the final part of the Battle Royale, when all the players start to concentrate in the same area.

- To collect resources for buildings, you can inspect the treasure chests as usual, but you also have a pickaxe with which you can destroy barrels, wooden floors, trees, and cars from which you can derive different types of materials. Pay attention, even in this case, to the sound factor: the adversaries will hear your noisy actions, which is why they will approach your position. Carefully take advantage of the situation, misleading those who are in the area.

Chapter 3
10 Golden Rules to Become a Pro

Rule #1 Hunter and prey

Moving around the map can be problematic: despite its "limited" size and the absence of vehicles, it is good to understand that moving requires attention and strategy. Try to avoid large spaces but use the obstacles and elements of the setting to conceal your presence and be less prone to ambushes or precision shots.

Rule #2 Play with Headphones

Whether you play in groups or not, using a good pair of headphones can make the difference. Fortnite's sound design is in fact developed to allow players to feel their own at different levels and in a more incisive way, so as to make it clear if anyone it is approaching or not. It's a great way to plan your next move!

Rule #3 Leave That Door Closed

Apparently, in Battle Royale, even a simple open door can become a strategic opportunity. It is usually good practice to close the doors if you enter the buildings, in this way you "suggest" that nobody has entered the building and you can surprise any explorers. Yet, the power of mental games here is so much: opening them all could be a warning, but also a misdirection to suggest that the house is empty and has simply been robbed.

Rule #4 Everyone Can Hear You Screaming on the Map

As we have already told you: sound is an integral part of the gameplay. Getting around is generally noisy and running without crouching, in addition to the sound, will also leave a trail behind you, making you more visible in the distance. So do not just listen to the way you are moving: crouch and sprint in that position. You will be slow but silent (more or less).

Rule #5 Jumping is a bit like Running Away

In your crossings for the map, in the vicinity of buildings or agglomerations, you will see tires: if you jump on it, you will be propelled upwards, such as to allow you to climb on the roofs of some buildings or simply to escape from a disadvantageous situation and make your tracks lose. And it's super fun!

Rule #6 All tastes + 1

To be sufficiently versatile and competitive in every situation, it is good to keep in mind that a varied arsenal will give you more chances of success. The weapons you ALWAYS want to have with you are the shotgun, the assault rifle, and the sniper rifle. They are fundamental starting points for your game and perfect for every situation.

Rule #7 Weapons and rarities

Destiny has done school and just like a role-playing game, even Fortnite has its own weapon rarity system: five to be exact. Gray is the most common, then green, blue, purple, and orange, which is the rarest tier. The rarer the weapon is, the more effective it is in inflicting damage.

Rule #8 Where to land?

With such a large map and 100 players to hunt down, decide where the map landed can be the basis for your strategy. Follow your teammates to get coverage or go solo, maybe preferring areas with the highest chance of loot, such as Haunted Hills or Junk Junction. In your first games, you will want to have more time available to understand the pace of play and get used to it.

We recommend you to prefer less "contested" areas, such as Flush Factory, and avoid places like Anarchy Acres.

Rule #9 Building Structures

One of the most interesting aspects of Fortnite is the ability to create simple structures and destroy (almost) everything you see: buildings, trucks, structures—everything can be torn to pieces and it is a great advantage if you can keep it in mind, especially in situations of an apparent "Mexican stalemate." Do not stay still in the same place for too long, that's for sure.

Rule #10 Bimbi-line Bling

The most famous of us have the opportunity to make a group with the well-known singer Drake, while the less fortunate individuals under the age of 12 delight in bawling without restraint in the microphone. If you want to avoid listening to the verses of American children with too much free time, turn off the in-game voice chat in the game options.

Chapter 4
The Best Places to Land

After giving you 10 Gold Tips on how to avoid an unpleasant start, it is good to face another important problem of experience: where do I land? In the battle royale genre, in fact, the players will be launched at high altitude on the map, where they will then have to land with a parachute in the place they prefer. The map is great, though, and not having a clear idea of what you're going to can be problematic and not fun at all.

Quite simply, landing in a very populated area, while giving you the ability to immediately get rare and important loot weapons, will expose you to enemies. That is that of experienced players, who probably have from their dozens of hours of play.

You are inexperienced and frightened by the world, so it is good to consider landing in a quieter area of the map that, although always dangerous, will allow you to make your way and have time to evaluate the opportunities as you continue. Wherever you land, however, it is good to keep in mind the sound, a tinkle, which indicates chests. If you hear a strange sound, immediately run to it to catch the high-level loot.

One of the most classic routes, for example, to maintain a good balance between loot and a not too populated area, is that of Junk Junction and Haunted Hills, and then to Pleasant Park. Not everyone chooses to land here and the different geographic conformances of places allow to get good loot without being too exposed to enemy raids.

Other places rather calm and with the necessary loot to allow you to survive are Flush Factory and Lonely Lodge. These are no places full of loot, but they could be for you and allow you to climb positions with less intense rhythms. Between these two places then, there is an abandoned shed containing a crate and in the vicinity several trees to store wood.

Dusty Depot could also be an excellent opportunity because in some games it does not receive many visits to the first landing and in its three structures, it often contains boxes and excellent objects. Moisty Mire is a virtually empty location where you will rarely find something but you will have the advantage of being on the edge of the map, so without the possibility of being attacked behind.

If you are looking for loot, you will want to land in Anarchy Acres, to the left of which is a Motel with a rather valuable loot. The problem is that there is so much competition so you will have to be quick and know how to move, otherwise, you will immediately be manure for the ground. An interesting strategy could be to approach the Motel from a distance, from abandoned houses and evaluate the situation.

As you can see from our wise words and arcane knowledge, knowing where to land can give you environmental and tactical advantages as well as in terms of gameplay purely depending on your style of play. Always try new approaches and find your balance, just so you will have fun without cursing unhealthy.

Haunted Hills

They are located in the northwest corner of the game map to the south of Junk Junction and to the west of Pleasant Park. Haunted Hills is a ruined place, with decadent cemeteries and a series of mausoleums. Once in the area, be sure to check the top of the tower at once: under the window's shelf, there is often a chest. Landing on it directly can also prove to be a winning strategy, as it will save you time and provide you with a not inconsiderable tactical advantage since from above you can control the area well and anticipate the moves of the enemies out of cover. It is also an excellent sniping point, provided you have a sniper rifle suitable for the purpose, of course.

If you happen to hear the coveted sound of chests while you walk around in the mausoleums, but you cannot find them even after having explored all the rooms nearby, do not worry. Most likely it will be well-hidden in an underground room under the floor. Another chest can often be found in a small enclosed grave in the northwest section of the hills.

Tilted Towers

Located to the south of Loot Lake, Tilted Towers is a settlement similar to a city full of tall buildings and towers. The abundance of structures makes the location extremely suitable for looting, and therefore extremely populated. Many players decide to venture into the buildings in the area, so if you decide to do so, make sure you are equipped to fight and respond to the enemy fire. The highest points of the structures are particularly coveted because they are suitable for sniping. As you try to get there, be careful where you put your feet since a fall from that height will result in certain death.

Exactly like on the Haunted Hills, here too you have the opportunity to land on the tallest building, the clock tower, where often there are one or two chests. You will almost certainly have to fight to get it, since it is a busy place, so you work well on your landing technique. To arrive first, of course, will provide you with a considerable advantage.

In the tunnel that runs under the city, there are two parked trucks, one of which hides a chest inside. In the other, however, you can find a wide variety of objects, so wandering around in this area can almost certainly find you a weapon, one way or another.

Snobby Shores

Snobby Shores is located at the westernmost point of the map, northwest of Greasy Grove. It is a luxury residential area comprising five different fenced houses. As you can easily guess,

193

they are all stuffed with loot and a theatre of close collisions, so be on guard when you venture into these properties.

We advise you to land in the house further north, as under the roof a chest is hidden, while two others are on the second floor: one under the stairs, and the other breaking the wall behind the table in the kitchen. The southernmost residence, however, hides an underground room that can hold up to three crates. To find it, enter the one-story building, enter the bedroom and destroy the closet. Behind it is the entrance to the bunker!

A box can be found immediately under the stairs (to take it, you will have to destroy another wardrobe), while the other two in a contiguous room easy to find.

Junk Junction

Junk Junction is a small landfill located just north of Haunted Hills with breakers, stacks of cars, and a giant crane. Being located in one of the corners of the game map, it can be an ideal choice for all players who prefer to avoid the most crowded areas in an attempt to circumvent and surprise the enemies behind.

The stacks of cars are excellent covers but do not forget to check their top, where you can find weapons and healing objects. The structures are also very close, so you do not need to use your building materials to create bridges between them, it will be enough to jump from one to another. Once you have checked them all out, take out your pickaxe and dismantle them from first to last to get a lot of metal to use to build.

In most cases, it is possible to find a chest in the orange car wrecker in the northernmost section of the area and another on the second floor of the building immediately in front of it.

Shifty Shafts

Shifty Shafts is a mining complex located in the southwest section of the map, between Tilted Towers (to the north), Greasy Grove (to the west), and Flush Factory (to the south), so it is an extremely crowded area that needs to be crossed quickly.

Once in the area, immediately check the white shed in the westernmost area of the area, since it almost always has a chest and several weapons. Landing at this point can be a winning strategy, as you will immediately take advantage of enemies in the area.

The mining tunnels are full of loot, so they tempt many players. We, therefore, recommend that you arm yourself with a shotgun. Given the nature of the area, you will almost certainly find yourself caught up in close combat. Your efforts will surely be rewarded because behind the destructible wooden walls are several chests.

Chapter 5

Let's Talk about Building

Building is an important part of the gameplay to the point that it could make the difference between a win and a loss. Mastering the controls is therefore fundamental both on PC and on consoles where it is naturally less immediate to juggle between the various commands and the various options. Doing it, or at least trying it, is already a half-win, so you can avoid offering yourself as a tribute as Hunger Games' Katniss during the first few minutes of the game.

How to build?

On PC

Q: It takes you to the construction menu or creates walls instantly

F1, F2, F3, F4: use them to move between the various construction options

F5: Used to place traps on flat surfaces

Right mouse button: In the construction menu, use it to change the material used

G: Use it to modify an already created structure, add doors, stairs, or a billy of the structure

A: Use it to rotate the structure

On PC, expert players tend to assign alternative keys to make their game more immediate and fast and to react to any eventuality in a short time. Basically, you have to become a Predator:

Walls: Q or E

Platforms: F or V

Ramps: F or V

PS4

[Circle]: Build menu

Hold [Circle]: Edit a structure

[Triangle]: To move in the construction menu

[Square]: Press to choose a trap, press and hold to interact, press and hold to go to the trap menu

[R1]: Rotate a structure

[R2]: Positions a structure

[L1]: Change the materials

[L2]: Equip the desired construction

[Right Analog]: Reset changes to a structure

Xbox One

[B]: Construction menu

Hold [B]: Change a structure

[Y]: To move in the construction menu

[X]: Press to choose a trap, press and hold to interact, press and hold to go to the trap menu

[RB]: Rotate a structure

[RT]: Positions a structure

[LB]: Change the materials

[LT]: Equip the desired construction

[Right Stick]: Reset changes to a structure

Pro commands?

The pro command option is relegated to console versions. They modify the traditional control scheme to offer something quite different, more in line with the philosophy of the PC version: more speed in building and changing weapons. It takes time to get used to it, but the road to becoming pro is dark and full of terror, especially on PS4 and Xbox One.

One of the features that made the gameplay of Fortnite so compelling than its opponents is the possibility of building fortifications. The world in which Fortnite Battle Royale is set can be destroyed and remodeled using its harvesting tool.

In the final stages of the game, it is very important to create points of advantage over the opponents and then be able to exploit their war power in the correct way. To do this, it is necessary to have a good command of the mechanics linked to the construction of buildings. It is important to know which materials are great for certain phases of the game, how to change your creations for your own purposes.

With this guide, we see specifically what the game world is made of and what type of construction we can achieve with what we did.

In the world of Fortnite, the three resources available through the harvesting tool are: wood, stone/brick, and metal. These three resources represent the fuel with which your character realizes and designs the fortifications.

Game resources are obtained using the harvesting tool on the objects in the Fortnite world and based on their appearance, the objects will give a different material. The best method to gain materials in the course of the game is to find particular objects that act as small resources mines.

For wood, for example, the best objects are trees and pallets; for stone, the best objects are the rock formations; and for metal, it is better to pick up cars or ferrous rocks. Each of these items will give our character a different amount of material depending on its size.

The largest trees of Fortnite, those inside Moisty Mire, donate up to 100 units of wood to the player who knocks them down.

The best place to be able to loot a lot of stone are the mines scattered around the game map; they have the form of inlets in the ground studded with small rocky monoliths that can give the player up to 50 stone units each.

Metal, given its strength and strength within the construction optics, has no real looting points. It should simply be collected wherever it is seen if you intend to build a lot of structures using this material.

When you harvest something, you have to pay attention to the blue circle that will appear above the polygonal model of the object in question: hitting this circle will double the damage and we will complete the collection of the desired resource more quickly.

The Harvesting Tool

- Each hit deals 10 damage to any players, and it is not possible to make a headshot and double the damage.
- Each hit deals 50 damage to any type of item not crafted by the player; if you hit the blue circle that appears after the first shot, the damage becomes 100.
- Each hit deals 25 damage to the objects created by the players; the damage becomes 50 if you hit the aforementioned blue circle.

What can we build in Fortnite?

Building structures are one of the cornerstones of Fortnite's gameplay. During the game, the structures will come to our aid so many times that after a few hours, the real potential will be fully understood. The speed of construction of the various structures depends on the type of material we have chosen.

To build, just access the special menu during their games. The menu consists of five different types of structures that can then be built with a simple click.

These structures are:

- Walls
- Floors/Ceilings
- Stairways
- Roofs
- Traps

They cost (traps excluded) 10 resources. It is possible to select the resource with which to build and it will influence the HP of the structure itself. During construction, you can choose the orientation of the structure using the R key.

Upon erecting a structure, it will appear with about half of its total HP, filling up in the next 5 seconds. It is possible to walk and modify the structures still under construction without problems of any kind.

You can edit your structures using the appropriate function. This will show a geometric grid that varies from structure to structure; by eliminating or modifying the number of squares present, it is possible to change the shape of your building by adding doors, windows or changing the vertical orientation (with regards to stairs and roofs).

If a resource is depleted during the construction of a structure and the "Automatic Material Change" option is active from the Options menu, your character will automatically change the resource type for the next structure.

Tips for building

- The stairs are to be built by sticking them between three walls. Doing so will reduce the possibility of being hit on the sides and will force the opponent to gain an advantage in height to break down.

- You can trap your opponent inside rock or metal walls to save time.

- By replacing walls, floors and ceilings inside houses, you can place traps in unexpected points and surprise your opponent.

Chapter 6
The Best Items to Use

Surviving in the battle of a hundred players requires an absolute knowledge of what you will shoot with and where you will shoot. Obviously, between a bullet and the other, it will be necessary to medicate one's wounds, lay deadly traps, or disguise themselves with bushes—not to pass the time but to increase once again their chances of survival.

These objects are of great importance within Fortnite because they allow the player to prolong his stay inside the island by equipping him with health, shield, or aids of various kinds.

Traps

Traps are one of the best ways to ambush enemies. They can be attached to walls, floors or ceilings. To select them, just use the building menu and select the slot (F5 on a computer) and then attach it as if it were any other construction.

The traps are found both inside the boxes and on the floors of numerous structures.

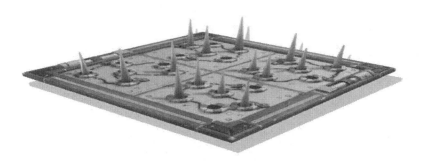

Damage Trap (Uncommon)

The basic trap: it can be placed on floors, walls, and ceilings to damage other players by surprise when they enter rooms or buildings. After the release of Patch 4.2, the damaging trap deals 75 damage if you stay above it for more than 1.5s.

They are a great way to fortify buildings during the early stages of the game. If the plane on which it rests is destroyed, it is also destroyed. You can place two traps in front of each other to deal up to 150 damage in a single moment, killing a good percentage of unwary enemies.

Launch Pad (Epic)

This is one of the most useful objects of the game as it allows the player and his friends to move very quickly in the open spaces. Jumping on it will propel you a large distance vertically, after which you may open your glider to land safely.

The launch pad is able to save a group of players from very risky situations if used correctly. You can simplify your life by placing it above a very high building, even if improvised. Even enemies can use the launch pad. The launch pad will wear out after 10 launches.

Cozy Campfire (Rare)

Like his trampoline friend, this object is aimed at helping the player prolonging his life. The Cozy Campfire is an enormously useful object because it takes care of 2HP per second for 25 seconds in the immediate surrounding area.

It is important to use this object correctly because all the players in their vicinity recover HP with each passing second. Placing a campfire inside a fort or a fortification keeping the surrounding areas under control is a great way to use it.

Another interesting choice is to place him in a fort during a prolonged fight, so as to benefit his team or his person with extra 50HP. It is possible to place two very close bonfires, doubling the rate of care.

Healing/Support Items

These are related to our character's shield and life statistics. You can pass them on to your peers using the inventory and the appropriate commands.

Shield Potions (Rare)

One of Fortnite's most important objects. It is possible to find it both on the ground and in the treasure chests as it increases the chances of survival during a firefight. It takes 5 seconds to drink this potion. This item gives you 50 shield points. You can get to 100 shield points by drinking this potion.

Small Shield Potion (Common)

It works in pretty much the same way as the aforementioned potion if it were not only offering 25 shield points. They are found both on the ground and in chests, in groups of 3 potions at a time. It takes 2 seconds to drink a small shield potion. By drinking small Shield Potions you can get a maximum 50 shield points, forcing the player to find other ways to complete the remaining 50 points.

Apple

One of the last objects added with the arrival of the very recent Patch 4.2, the apples are fruits present near the bushes that can be used by pressing the action button (E on the PC) able to restore 5 HP to the user. Consuming an apple takes a single second and you can bring your HP to 100 simply by eating them.

Mushroom

Object added with the Patch 4.3. The mushroom is the equivalent of the apple with regards to shields. It is found in the woods and in the grasslands, in correspondence to humid or dark places. It can be consumed by pressing the action key (E on the PC) and is able to restore 5 shield points to the user. Consuming a mushroom takes one second and with it you can bring your shield to 100, bypassing the limits imposed by the small shield potion.

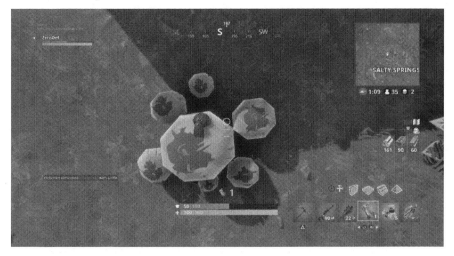

Bandages

One of the most common objects found inside Fortnite, practically in every chest and in every floor. The bandages are the lowest step of the healing items in the title, giving the player 15HP at a time with a usage time of 4 seconds. Using the bandages, it will be possible to heal up to a maximum of 75HP. They are found in packs of 4 units.

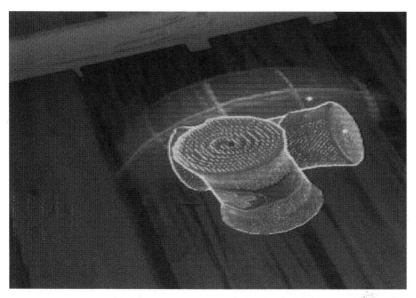

Med Kit (Uncommon)

The Med Kit is the next step to the bandages. This first aid box needs 10 seconds to be used by the player but heals to 100 health points, always bringing the user's health to the maximum. It can be found both on the ground and inside crates or distributors.

Chug Jug (Legendary)

100 health points, 100 shield points, and 15 seconds to consume the potion. The Chug Jug is the definitive healing item, able to heal everything that is not yet dead back up to its maximum health and shields. The Chug Jug has the defect of being particularly rare and its long time of consumption. If anything, you should not intend to use this item during a firefight try to fortify yourself in the best possible way.

Slurp Juice (Epic)

Slurp Juice is an all-around item. It restores 25 health points and 25 shield points over 25 seconds avoiding any kind of limitation. Consuming a Slurp Juice takes 2 seconds. Only one Slurp Juice can be activated at a time.

Bush (Legendary)

The bush is one of the funniest objects in the entire game. It is worn by using it as a potion or a bandage in three seconds and gives the character the identity of a self-propelled shrub. If you crouch while wearing the bush, you are extremely difficult to spot. It is useful if accompanied by a sniper rifle or long distance weapons, it allows you to get some kills without being discovered if used with the right timing and in the right environment.

While you are disguised as a bush, it will be possible to do all the actions an undisguised player can do. The bush will disappear if you take damage from any source, storm and fall damage included.

The backpacks are the latest arrivals, which landed with the same patch that brought the solid gold mode v2. They occupy an inventory slot and can be moved to different places; you can have only one backpack in your inventory at a time, as picking a new one will replace the one currently in use.
Let's see what backpacks exist in the world of Fortnite.

Jetpack (Legendary)

Bring the battle in the clouds. The first of a new type of object: the jetpack.

The description of the Jetpack and the historical memory attached to the name itself already announces sparks. This backpack will allow the player to fly around the playing area in an almost unlimited way. Once in flight, it will be possible to do almost (you cannot use the close-up aim) everything. The Jetpack is of legendary rarity and is only found within the treasure chests.

The Jetpack has a bar, visible both in-game and the object selection menu, which indicates how long it can be used. This bar is exhausted by flying or activating the backpack. You can fly with the Jetpack or more generally activate it by pressing the jump button while in mid-air; the Jetpack recharges very slowly when it is not in use. Once the bar has been completely worn, it will break.

If you activate the Jetpack while falling from high heights, you can nullify any fall damage with the right timing. It is also extremely useful to run away when you are inside the storm due to its ability to make obstacles simple to climb over.

The strength of the Jetpack is in giving the close encounters based on shotguns or slow pistols (revolver, hand cannons) a new type of rhythm. The increase in mobility allows the player to deceive and find new glimpses from which to impale the unfortunate opponent. To do this, just use the Jetpack that little enough to get a little 'push and disorient the opponent. It is not recommended to use the Jetpack for long and medium distances.

Chapter 7
Challenges

Fortnite Challenges can be completed during Battle Royale games. In this chapter, we will explain what they consist of, how to complete them and we will propose you the new challenges that are launched every week.

In addition to the natural business of surviving as long as possible during a game, there are also other activities to which you can devote, which can vary from case to case: for example, using a specific weapon or consuming a particular object, or even finding hidden objects. All these activities give you extra XP points and increase the Battle Stars.

Guide to the Weekly and Daily Challenges of Fortnite

Every 24 hours, new Daily Challenges are offered in Fortnite. These ask you to complete certain objectives, such as killing a certain amount of opponents or with a certain type of weapon, and once completed will guarantee you some prizes.

You can check these challenges every day in the lobby, and by clicking on the related entries you will have access to the specific details of each challenge.

The Weekly Challenges, instead, appear in the relevant section, with a table at the top of the screen. These are exclusive to the owners of the Battle Pass.

Every week, therefore, there will be a new set of challenges, and even though many of them are intuitive, we still offer a quick explanation of the kind of challenges you might find:

- Action-Based Challenges - Use a specific weapon, tool, or tactic a certain number of times throughout the many parts (does not need to be completed in one game) until you unlock it. This is undoubtedly the easiest kind of challenge since you can devote yourself throughout the season.

- Challenges based on Location - You will need to find a specific point on the map, helping you with only a vague clue. These are usually well-hidden, but it's nothing really impossible. We will, however, help you to find them all in our guide.

- Finding chests - These challenges will ask you to find and open some boxes located within a specific map. It will be impossible to complete this challenge in a single game, so dedicate yourself to research during the arc of more matches. It will also be easier to complete these challenges weeks later than the arrival of the challenge, given that a new challenge will be proposed with a different location that will immediately become popular, leaving you more room for the old challenge.

It is important to underline that it is not necessary to complete the Weekly Challenges within seven days of their appearance, but they can be completed before the end of the Season. This means that you can dedicate yourself to challenges of several weeks at the same time, for a greater variety in the gaming experience.

Week 2 Challenges of Season 4:

Search for treasure chests in Greasy Grove (0/7)

Use the Pop Rocks (0/7)

Damage enemies with silenced weapons (0/500)

Dance in front of several cameras (0/7)

Search between a scarecrow, a pink car and a big screen - Hard (0/1)

Eliminate enemies with explosive weapons - Hard (0/3)

Eliminate enemies in Tomato Town - Hard (0/3)

Apparently, there are no "breaks" for the many Fortnite players who, starting tomorrow, will be able to try their hand at new challenges. The first 4, upon their completion, will guarantee 5 Battle Stars, while the others will be 10, due to the higher difficulty level.

Week 3 Challenges of Season 4

Watch the Replay of a Match - 5 stars

Inflict damage to opponents with guns - 5 stars

Look for treasures in the Lonely Lodge - 5 stars

Search for Rubber ducks - 5 stars

Follow the map of the treasure found in Tomato Town (Hard) - 10 stars

Week 4 Challenges of Season 4

Deal damage to opponents with the SMG (500)

Search Treasure in Dusty Depot (7)

Use a Jetpack (1)

Search for Gravity Stones (7)

Follow the treasure map found in Wailing Woods – Difficult

Eliminate opponents with Minigun or LMG (2) - Difficult

Eliminate opponents at Lucky Landing (3) – Difficult

Week 8 Challenges

Use a vending machine - 5 Stars: The new vending machines allow you to exchange resources for weapons and objects.

Inflict 1000 points of damage to your opponents with explosive weapons - 5 Stars: The explosive weapons already do them a lot of damage, so you will not get too long to reach your goal. All you need is the guided missiles, the grenade launcher, the remote control explosives and the expensive old grenades to reach the 1000 damage points.

Search for treasure chests at Snobby Shores - 5 Stars: Simply go to the Snobby Shores and look for 7 treasure chests to complete this challenge.

Dance on different dance floors - 5 Stars: You will have to use the dance emote on three different dance floors. Soon we will attach a practical map to find them all.

Look for the treasure among three boats - 10 Stars: Another week, another treasure hunt. Here is a video guide to find the treasure.

Eliminate enemies with assault rifles (Hard) - 10 Stars: To complete this challenge you will have to eliminate 5 opponents using the assault rifle.

Eliminate your opponents in Moldy Warehouse - 10 Stars

Week 9 Challenges

Through reliable leaks, the Week 9 challenges were discovered early. Remembering that they may be subject to some change in their official release, we propose them below, so as to be ready as soon as they start.

As usual, there will be 7 challenges that will reward players, available only to those who have purchased the Battle Pass of Season 3. The week 9 will be the penultimate of the season, which will end with the challenges of the week 10. These will probably ask to fly inside the rings that appeared in the skies of Fortnite.

Damage to enemy structures - 5 Stars: you only need to deal 5,000 damage to enemy structures to earn 5 deserved Stars.

Find the crates in the Haunted Hills - 5 Stars: there are 7 hidden coffers in the Haunted Hills, find them all and the Stars will be yours.

Build structures - 5 Stars: structures are the daily bread for every Fortnite player, engine 250 will complete the challenge.

Visit Taco stores in a single match - 5 Stars: visit 3 Taco stores in one game and unlock the challenge.

Follow the treasure map to Moisty Mire - 10 Stars: the treasure hunt of the week is set in Moisty Mire, complete it and you will receive 10 Stars.

Shotgun kills - 10 stars: you only need to eliminate 5 opponents with a shotgun to gain the beauty of 10 Stars.

Eliminating adversaries - 10 Stars: to complete this challenge you will have to kill 3 enemies at Adventure Landing.

How to complete the Challenges of Week 8 in Fortnite
Here is a list of the Weekly Challenges of Season 3 of Fortnite (in the update).

Week 10 Challenges

Look for chests in the Fatal Fields (7)

Damage with headshots to opponents (250)

Search for trunks in different areas with names (Tilted Towers, Fused Conduits, etc.) (12)

Parachute through floating rings (10)

Look for a Circle of Stones, a Wooden Bridge and a red camper (1) Difficult

Eliminate opponents (10) Difficult

Eliminate opponents in Pleasant Park (3) Difficult

When are the Fortnite Daily and Weekly Challenges reset? On what day and at what time?

Daily Challenges (available to all players) are reset to 1.01 CEST (Europe)

Weekly Challenges (available only to holders of the Battle Pass) will be released EVERY THURSDAY at 10 am (CEST)

Chapter 8
How to Fight like a Champion

The most well-known mode of Fortnite is certainly Battle Royale. In this period, thanks to the wide success of the genre with titles like H1Z1 or the more recent PUBG, Fortnite has rapidly increased, thanks to the free-to-play nature of the title. Here are some tips to start this mode and not be so lost.

Choose the options that best suit your style

While waiting for the bus to launch you down into the map, access the settings. The most interesting parameter to change will be that of sensitivity. A key factor in a game like this. If you are a beginner to this genre, try to keep a low sensitivity otherwise you will have difficulty to aim. On the contrary, if you are a veteran, increase it as much as possible so that you can move the view faster and have faster reaction times. If you are on pc, take a look at the graphics settings. In games like these, which require a high level of competitiveness, the frames per second are a fundamental component. There will also be some options that will simplify your life during the exploration. Take a look at them and decide if they can bother you or not.

Avoid crowded areas

Once you have exited the Battlebus, you will have to use a parachute to land in the area that most suits you. Try to run into areas with few players and get off as fast as possible. It will be important in the first moments of play to collect as much as possible, and in crowded areas, you will find opponents who will try to steal from you as much as possible and at the first opportunity will hit you from behind.

Pay attention to the details

Try to get headphones and listen carefully to what's going on around you. Steps, explosions, blows. Every sound will be vital. Close the doors behind you and watch the open ones. It means that someone has already been in the building and there may still be waiting for you. Do not stay too long in large areas and with few shelters. Your goal will be to stay as covered as possible. So, in case they identify you, you can hide as soon as possible and, if the situation proves favorable, prepare for the counterattack.

Create new strategies

The beauty of this kind of game is being able to take advantage of the environment that surrounds you and play in the way you like best. For example, you can play aggressive and then try to kill as many people as possible, attracting them to you and showing you they're helpless. Or you can be more on the defensive, hiding as much as possible and avoiding any clashes. Remember that in the game, there will be many useful tools for your purposes, such as traps or shields.

Learn to know the weapons

Each weapon in Fortnite will be marked with a color. Each color will indicate the rarity that in increasing order will be: grey, green, blue, purple, and gold. Assault rifles will be the most versatile in battle, but our advice is to try as much as possible to have a balanced weaponry, with weapons both for close combat and for wider distances. Even the grenades and rocket launchers will be very useful, so do not disdain them. You can use them mainly to destroy guards and buildings and leave your enemies uncovered.

Chapter 9
The Players to Avoid and How to Recognize Them

To survive Fortnite storms, you need to know what types of people you can trust

Fortnite was born as a cooperative survival game, although it recently released a mode strongly influenced by the popular PlayerUnknown's Battlegrounds, in which half of the world's population was turned into brainless mutant zombies and your goal is to save humanity by trying to survive the waves of enemies. Inside the game, it is possible to build fortresses, use powerful skills and recently also fight against 99 other players in a challenge to the death. As in many other multiplayer games, during your adventures you will meet all kinds of players, so we have prepared a quick guide to the 10 types of players that you absolutely must avoid on Fortnite.

The Architect

Distinctive trait: Obsessive-compulsive constructor
It is usually found: several meters above the ground
If you start building you will see it arrive. But if you do not build at all, you will see it arrive and build in your place. The architect takes the defense of the base very seriously, he thinks there is nothing more important than adding yet another balcony to his fortress. Sometimes he builds an endless ramp for no apparent

reason, and often we would like him to put down the carpenter's tools to pick up a rifle and help with the dirty work.

The Sportsman

Distinctive trait: Love to make a corset

It is usually found: Always on the move

The sportsman often goes out for a walk, and he spends a lot of time letting himself be fascinated by the beauty of the world around him. You let yourself get a little bit of here and a little bit of it, popping up every so often over the horizon. The problem is that between a farming session and a secondary goal it's never where it should be, and eventually, you get used to playing without it.

The Lunatic

Distinctive trait: Unjustified fear of losing something

It is usually found: To fight against a monster

This player is out of his mind, he throws his head down to anything that moves and when there is to reach a goal always takes the most direct route, regardless of the danger of the situation. His favorite weapon is the sword, brandished with a strange grin on his face. When he plays Battle Royale he never has a precise plan, he simply aims to get instant gratification in every way possible.

The Ballast

Distinctive trait: It will make you die

It is usually found: Near certain death

Perhaps it is better to keep the distance from the ballast, nine times out of ten you will accidentally lock yourself inside a wall. This is the type of player who accidentally builds ladders that the monsters can use to launch themselves in the middle of your base. Then activate Atlas too soon, you lose in the map just when the fight is about to begin and at the precise moment when you see it appear on the horizon is chased by an army of mutants ready to destroy everything you've just created.

The FPS patient

Distinctive trait: Think about being on CoD
It is usually found: To play CoD
He does not care what Fortnite's peculiarities are, nor does the other players expect anything from him. He does not want to waste time understanding the statistics, classes, constructions or defense strategies in the game: the FPS patient just wants to aim and shoot (sometimes throw a grenade). For this you usually find him playing the Soldier class, constantly looking for new ammunition and mutants to rid of shots.

The Competitive

Distinctive trait: Plays only Battle Royale
It is usually found: On top of another 99 bodies
Before the introduction of the Battle Royale mode, Fortnite was a tower defense shooter with a solid cooperative component. But the Competitive player does not remember since it spends

its time exclusively looking for opponents to be defeated in PvP. Down with the team play and the construction of impregnable fortresses, who cares about the objectives and levels? Not this player evidently, he just wants to remain the only survivor of the game.

The Bulldozer

Distinctive trait: Hates the environment that surrounds it
It is usually found: To break things
Even if the game allows you to crumble anything that surrounds you, it does not mean you should spend 100% of your time doing it. But the Bulldozer does not want to hear it and continues undaunted with its methodical devastation of the scenarios, perhaps it simply has the repressed anger to vent, or loves to collect screws and bolts. In any case, the Bulldozer cannot come to help you with the defense of the base at this time, it is too busy in the extermination of all that can be broken.

The Hunter

Distinctive trait: a Cold-blooded murderer
It is usually found: Hidden in the bushes
The hunter is a professional in what he does. Not content with simply defending his base or taking out the waves of mutants that appear nearby, the hunter goes straight to the source of problems equipped with a crossbow, a sniper rifle and a samurai sword to take out until the last threat present in the

level. In PvP mode, it is particularly lethal, a force of nature that wants at all costs to hang your head on the wall like a trophy.

The Sadist

Distinctive trait: Love the traps, perhaps a little too much
It is usually found: Waiting for the next prey
In the event of an unlikely invasion of zombies, mutants or aliens, the ability to prepare traps to defend the territory is quite important. Home security would be the top priority for many people and could give us the chance to fight on equal terms with the invaders. But some people carry this concept to the extreme, preparing endless labyrinths in which to watch their adversaries burn, explode and electrify, and then spend whole minutes waiting for the next victim to make the worst decision of his life.

The Perfectionist

Distinctive trait: His passion is ticking off items from the lists
It is usually found: Wherever there is a secondary objective
Fortnite is not just about zombies and fortresses, there are also goals that can provide a fair amount of experience points and equipment. Most can be safely ignored and some reappear indefinitely. Unfortunately, however, there are some players who just cannot ignore secondary missions and chase any notification appearing on their interface. You may have entered the game to do a quick mission, perhaps before dinner, but the perfectionist has another idea in mind. If in the same game you

find him, the architect and the bulldozer, maybe it's better if you bring the plate to the screen.

Chapter 10
From Good to Great, 10 Tips That Will Make You a Pro

1. Always take time to accumulate resources

At the beginning of each level, you will have several minutes available to explore the area and stock up on useful materials. Take this time to destroy the objects you find on the road and fill your backpack with raw materials and construction materials. Make sure you always have enough screws and bolts to build ammo and traps: you can find them inside toolboxes or destroy mechanical and electrical objects, such as automobiles, generators and industrial equipment. If you are really short of resources you can even decide to create a private game, fill your pockets until they burst and then exit the level without completing the main objective: the materials will remain in your inventory even in the following games.

2. The most precious chests are at the top of the buildings

Given that you will spend a lot of time farming resources and raw materials, it is good to know how to optimize your time in the most efficient way: some of the rarest (and useful) materials in the game are found in special chests placed in the most inaccessible places of levels such as cellars, the floors, the terraces and the mines: we advise you to always keep the eyes (and ears) open for this kind of objects. They are surrounded by a slight glimmer, especially when they are in the darkest places and emit a sound clue that will help you to identify them even through ceilings and walls. If you do not have time to waste, we advise you to build a high platform and begin to sift the roofs of the buildings.

3. Defend the goal but do not overdo it

During the first 15/20 levels of the game, it does not make much sense to place the traps around the target: firearms and hero abilities are more than enough to defend the hot zone from waves of enemies. Build only the bare minimum to slow down the zombies and protect the area from projectiles. Also, make sure you never exceed the maximum number of buildings indicated by the objectives. The grade of the coins obtained will decide the quality of the end-level rewards.

4. Do not become attached to a single character

At the beginning of the game, it is very easy to become attached to a single character and invest all the experience gained on him. However, as the days pass, you will find that many missions will ask you to play specific heroes to receive their rewards. Always try to keep at least one character available for each class and distribute the experience points you earn fairly. The progression of the heroes is limited by the skill tree, so sooner or later you will still have to wait to unlock the nodes needed to further advance the level.

5. Level up the projects you use the most

In Fortnite, practically everything can be advanced, and projects for the creation of weapons and traps are certainly not less. The level of the project indicates the effectiveness that a given instrument will have in combat: this is why it is important to invest in the projects that will be used in-game. During the first hours of play, we recommend investing in firearms because the traps are more expensive to create and have less impact on the games. In addition, try to always carry around at least one weapon dedicated to melee: the game never warns you in advance when you are about to stay dry ammunition.

6. Create a team to tackle the most challenging missions

At the top of the main menu, there is a number that indicates the level of the general power of your character and consequently the level of missions that you should face. Contrary to what you might think, however, this level does not depend on the heroes you will use in battle or on their level, but on the quality of the survivors, you will assign to the teams in the appropriate section. The greater the level of the survivors, and the synergy between their personalities, the greater the overall level of player strength: make sure to assign the right survivors to the right role according to their specialty.

7. Keep traps for your base

Another important element to develop in order to progress in the game is the basic house: an instance in which the player has absolute control over traps and constructions that will have to be gradually improved to face waves of increasingly numerous and fierce monsters. In our opinion, this is the best place to invest the most precious traps offered by the game, also because it will not always be possible to find players who will help you defend your base. Keep aside the strongest traps you find in the levels and from time to time come back home to place them at the strategic points of your base (usually the perimeter of the stations is the best place).

8. Put duplicates in the sticker album

Almost all elements of the game can be destroyed in exchange for experience points or random projects, but duplicates also have another useful feature: they can be consumed to advance the album in the main menu. Each new grade provides the player with respectable rewards and at the beginning of the game, this is a great way to get llamas and resources. But be very careful not to waste useful projects: once confirmed the assignment you will not be able to go back.

9. Keep an eye on the most profitable missions

In the assignments section, there are many missions to be carried out individually within the levels of the game, some of which reappear at the same time every day. These missions, as well as being a nice diversion, provide valuable points to buy the special containers in the shape of a blade (yes, the animal) that provide rewards of all kinds and rarities. Set your style of play around these missions and you'll see that you'll never need to spend a single penny.

10. Send your heroes on missions and clear the search points

Last but not the least are the expeditions and research points, both linked to the passing of time in real life. Shipments are timed missions that serve to keep the heroes occupied that you do not intend to use in battle: they can provide precious materials or rare items, so it's important to make sure you never leave any vehicle stationary in the garage. Search points are a resource that is generated by the game every minute, even when you are not playing, which unfortunately has a maximum capacity limit. They can be "cashed out" to make room for new search points or invested on the nodes of the dedicated card to get bonuses and upgrades.

Chapter 11
A look at the weapons

During Fortnite games, an excellent strategy can make the difference between an embarrassing defeat and a glorious victory, but there is also something else you should always keep in mind: the choice of weapons! There are many scattered within the game map, all very different and in a sense unique.

In the beginning, however, indecision can reign supreme and it is really hard to know if the rifle that has just fallen at your feet is better or less than what you have in inventory. Speaking of every single weapon would be a titanic enterprise, but with this guide, we will try to come to meet you by describing those that we believe are the best currently available in the game.

Revolver

The Revolver is not hard to find and is often shelved by a certain type of player. In the right hands, however, it can become extremely effective, both short and medium distance. Thanks to the high damage he can score, even in the common variant he may be able to take out enemies with just two well-placed shots, often even one if he is already injured.

Common: DPS 48 | Damage 54 | Magazine 6

Uncommon: DPS 51 | Damage 57 | Magazine 6

Rare: DPS 54 | Damage 60 | Magazine 6

Assault Rifle (M16)

Without a doubt one of the best common weapons to take with you, suitable for most occasions. It is perfect for close and middle distance combat, given that if you use it accurately, the good firepower allows you to shoot down enemies quickly. On the long distance, however, begins to go difficulty due to the dispersion of the bullets, even more, accentuated if you hold the trigger. In these cases, you can remedy by shooting short bursts, rather than prolonged or moving to a more suitable weapon.

Common: DPS 176 | Damage 30 | Magazine 30

Uncommon: DPS 181 | Damage 33 | Magazine 30

Rare: DPS 192.5 | Damage 35 | Magazine 30

Pump Shotgun

The shotgun has a very low rate of fire, but the well-placed shots inflict a huge amount of damage (90/95), almost sufficient to take out an enemy at the height of life. Cold blood and correct positioning are essential, since missing the target could put you in a bad situation.

Uncommon: DPS 63 | Damage 90 | Magazine 5

Rare: DPS 66.5 | Damage 95 | Magazine 5

Tactical Shotgun

The tactical shotgun is probably one of the most important weapons in the game. It does less damage than the shotgun, but has a higher rate of fire and is effective from a shorter distance.

It is not uncommon to come across opponents who go around hopping and firing as hard as I can. They are annoying, but you can do it too!

Common: DPS 100 | Damage 67 | Magazine 8

Uncommon: DPS 105 | Damage 70 | Magazine 8

Rare: DPS 111 | Damage 74 | Magazine 8

Bolt-Action Sniper Rifle

A sniper rifle in your inventory can exponentially increase your chances of winning. Only one well-placed shot is needed to get rid of the enemies. Furthermore, the importance of sniper rifles increases with the progress of the game and with the decrease of competitors. As the match progresses, one-on-one clashes become more frequent, and in these, it is advisable to find a good vantage point from which to control the situation with your trusty sniper rifle. There are semi-automatic variants, but probably the best is the single shot Bolt-Action, which is devastating if used properly. Remember: patience, precision, and good positioning are the keys to success.

Rare: DPS 34.7 | Damage 105 | Magazine 1

Epic: DPS 36.3 | Damage 110 | Magazine 1

Legendary: DPS 38.3 | Damage 116 | Magazine 1

Rocket Launcher

A lot of power and a large area of effect, the rocket launchers hardly need any introduction. However, in certain situations, they could prove to be much more useful as instruments rather than weapons. Nothing prevents you from firing rockets on enemies (better if in groups, of course), but this category of weapons is very useful to destroy the buildings of others and to bring out those who until a moment before believed to be safe.

Rare: DPS 80 | Damage 110 | Magazine 1

Epic: DPS 85 | Damage 116 | Magazine 1

Legendary: DPS 90 | Damage 121 | Magazine 1

Assault Rifle (SCAR)

It's definitely the best weapon of the game right now. The SCAR assault rifle is the older brother of the M16 and can only be found in the Epic and Legendary variants: appellations that are fully deserving. Apparently, it looks like a normal weapon, but it is perfect in every situation, it is effective from every distance, it is precise and inflicts a considerable amount of damage. What do you want more? Maybe just a little 'luck, since it is not easy to find it: explore the map well and take out the enemies to have the privilege of getting their hands on a SCAR.

Epic: DPS 203.5 | Damage 37 | Magazine 30

Legendary: DPS 214.5 | Damage 39 | Magazine 30

Boogie Bomb

The Boogie bomb is an explosive weapon of rare quality that shares with the grenades the mode of use, but causes a very different effect! All enemies in the blast radius are forced to dance for 5 seconds, or until they receive damage. In that time frame, they cannot build, shoot or use items. It requires precision and a good timing calculation, but it is very fun to use (it very closely resembles the Ratchet & Clank Discotron) and is capable of reversing the fates of the clashes in an instant. They are on the battlefield individually, but you can carry up to 10 of them.

Conclusion

Thank you for making it through to the end of *Fortnite Battle Royale: Advanced Tips, Tricks and Map Strategies from Elite Players to WIN #1 VICTORY ROYALE!* Let's hope it was informative and able to provide you with all of the tools you need to achieve your goals whatever it is that they may be. Just because you've finished this book doesn't mean there is nothing left to learn on the topic, expanding your horizons is the only way to find the mastery you seek.

The next step is to stop reading and to get starting doing whatever it is that you need to do in order to ensure that you will be able to defend yourself in a Fortnite game. If you find that you still need help getting started, you will likely have better results by creating a schedule that you hope to follow including strict deadlines for various parts of the tasks as well as the overall completion of your preparations.

Studies show that complex tasks that are broken down into individual pieces, including individual deadlines, have a much greater chance of being completed when compared to something that has a general need of being completed but no real timetable for doing so. Even if it seems silly, go ahead and set your own deadlines for completion, complete with indicators of success and failure. After you have successfully completed all of your required preparations you will be glad you did.

Once you have finished your initial preparations it is important to understand that they are just that, only part of a larger plan of preparation. Your best chances for overall success will come by taking the time to learn as many Fortnite skills as possible. Only by using your prepared status as a springboard to greater preparation will you be able to truly rest soundly knowing that you are prepared for anything and everything that this game decides to throw at you.

Finally, if you found this book useful in any way, a review on Amazon is always appreciated!

Learn the latest tricks and tips while you play!

Get this this 3 book 1 bundle complete audiobook for absolutely **FREE**, and get access to Underground Tips & Secrets To Become a Fortnite God & Win Battle Royale LIKE THE PRO'S!

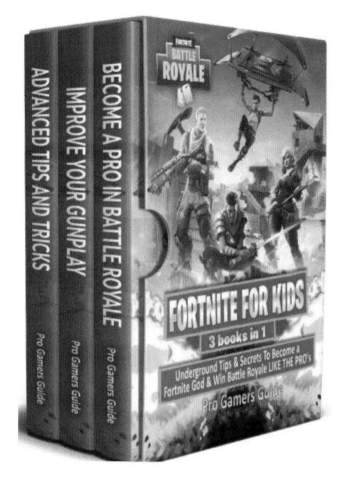

Download it for free: adbl.co/2PQHdX3